# INTERCULTURAL MARRIAGE

# Intercultural Marriage

## A PASTORAL GUIDE TO THE SACRAMENT

SIMON C. KIM &
RICKY MANALO, CSP

Paulist Press
New York / Mahwah, NJ

The Scripture quotations contained herein are from the New Revised Standard Version: Catholic Edition, Copyright © 1989 and 1993, by the Division of Christian Education of the National Council of the Churches of Christ in the United States of America. Used by permission. All rights reserved.

**Psalm 33/34: Taste and See** Vietnamese text and music © 1983, 2009, Đồng Dao. Published by OCP. All rights reserved. English: Rufino Zaragoza, OFM; Spanish verses adapted by Eleazar Cortés. English text, Spanish verses text and music © 2009, 2010, Rufino Zaragoza, OFM. Published by OCP. All rights reserved. Spanish refrain text © 1970, Conferencia Episcopal Española. All rights reserved. Used with permission.

Cover art: *La Sagrada Familia* by Ryan Aristotle A. Carreon. Used by permission of the artist.
Cover design by Joe Gallagher
Book design by Lynn Else

Copyright © 2022 by Simon C. Kim and Ricky Manalo, CSP

All rights reserved. No part of this publication may be reproduced, stored in a retrieval system, or transmitted in any form or by any means, electronic, mechanical, photocopying, recording, scanning, or otherwise, without either the prior written permission of the Publisher, or authorization through payment of the appropriate per-copy fee to the Copyright Clearance Center, Inc., www.copyright.com. Requests to the Publisher for permission should be addressed to the Permissions Department, Paulist Press, permissions@paulistpress.com.

Library of Congress Cataloging-in-Publication Data
Names: Kim, Simon C., author. | Manalo, Ricky, author.
Title: Intercultural marriage : a pastoral guide to the sacrament / Simon C. Kim & Ricky Manalo, CSP.
Description: New York / Mahwah, NJ : Paulist Press, [2022] | Includes bibliographical references and index. | Summary: "This book starts with a theological background of the lived intercultural realities of sacramental marriage within the larger context of our globalized world and then offers practical ways to deal pastorally with this challenge"— Provided by publisher.
Identifiers: LCCN 2021028205 (print) | LCCN 2021028206 (ebook) | ISBN 9780809154067 (paperback) | ISBN 9781587687839 (ebook)
Subjects: LCSH: Marriage—Religious aspects—Catholic Church.
Classification: LCC BX2250 .K45 2022 (print) | LCC BX2250 (ebook) | DDC 234/.165—dc23
LC record available at https://lccn.loc.gov/2021028205
LC ebook record available at https://lccn.loc.gov/2021028206

ISBN 978-0-8091-5406-7 (paperback)
ISBN 978-1-58768-783-9 (e-book)

Published by Paulist Press
997 Macarthur Boulevard
Mahwah, New Jersey 07430
www.paulistpress.com

Printed and bound in the
United States of America

In memory of Robert Schreiter, CPpS (1947–2021),
who taught the world how to appreciate intercultural theology.
And to Mark Francis, CSV, who continues to teach us how to
appreciate the intercultural dimensions of liturgy and worship.

# Contents

Foreword *by Rev. Mark R. Francis, CSV* .................................................... ix

Preface: Toward an Intercultural Approach to the Sacrament
 of Marriage ........................................................................................ xi

Acknowledgments ........................................................................................ xix

Chapter One: Vatican II Milestone: From Monocultural to
 Multicultural to Intercultural ............................................................ 1

Chapter Two: In Good Times and in Bad: Setting the
 Context for Intercultural Marriage .................................................... 9
 *Ethnographic Notes by Ricky Manalo, CSP*

Chapter Three: For Richer or for Poorer: Pastoral Approaches
 for Preparing Engaged Couples ........................................................ 27
 *Ethnographic Notes by Simon C. Kim*

Chapter Four: To Have, to Hold, and to Celebrate:
 Liturgical Interculturality in the Wedding of Melissa Hoang
 and Roberto Gonzales ........................................................................ 52
 *Ethnographic notes by Ricky Manalo, CSP*

Chapter Five: From This Day Forward: Interculturality as an
 Eschatological Sign ............................................................................ 66

Conclusion: Look Now with Favor on These Your Servants .................... 80

Appendix A: Cultural Influences ................................................................ 83

## Contents

Appendix B: A House of Prayer for All Peoples: Matrimony between Catholics and Baptized Non-Catholics ............................ 85

Notes ................................................................................. 91

Index ................................................................................ 103

About the Authors ............................................................ 106

# Foreword

This book would not have been needed sixty years ago. In pastoral practice before Vatican II, the marriage rite of the Western Catholic Church was largely "set in stone" as were the church laws surrounding how the celebration could take place if the bride and groom were not both Catholic. In Europe and North America it varied little from place to place. This was true even if the couple came from different cultural backgrounds. While there were some local cultural variations considered "quaint" by many European American groups, their incorporation would usually not have been considered because the instances of "mixed" culture marriages between Euro-Americans and people of other religious and cultural backgrounds were very rare.

Needless to say, times have changed. This book by Frs. Simon Kim and Ricky Manalo should be required reading for anyone involved today with marriage preparation, especially those charged with preparing wedding celebrations in parishes transformed by increasingly widespread cultural diversity. As theologian Karl Rahner famously stated, one of the principal achievements of the Second Vatican Council was the realization that we truly belong to a "world church." This means that we must take seriously the fact that Christianity is not tied exclusively to western European cultures, but that all cultures are worthy to "incarnate" the gospel. For this reason, our worship needs to reflect the cultural lenses with which we look at the world. The authors, using their unique Asian American lenses, offer a realistic and effective process designed to help couples from diverse cultural backgrounds think about and prepare for their weddings. They also offer valuable theological reflections on a renewed notion of sacramentality that underscores and supports the practical aspects of preparing an intercultural marriage rite.

Not surprising, crucial to their approach is a method that is not top-down but really bottom-up. They start with an activity that the church has not been particularly good at for many centuries: *listening*. Not only do they listen to the experience of several intercultural couples as they describe how these couples negotiated many of the challenges posed by their different cultural backgrounds, they also are attentive to their own cultural location as celibate priests from Asian American families. While knowledgeable of the theology and traditions of the church, their presentation is informed by the study of the intersection between the received Catholic tradition and the multiple aspects of the cultures present in an intercultural marriage.

This book appears at a vital moment in the life of the church in the United States. While it does not pretend to present all the answers to intercultural marriages, it offers something even more important: the right questions.

Rev. Mark R. Francis, CSV<br>
Professor of Liturgy<br>
Catholic Theological Union at Chicago

# Preface

## *Toward an Intercultural Approach to the Sacrament of Marriage*

CULTURAL HUMILITY, not humiliation, is the foundation for any healthy relationship, regardless of ethnicities, between individuals and society as a whole. Unfortunately, many who were the first to come to this country encountered both humility and humiliation, though this land of opportunity welcomed those far and wide. The welcoming encounters that families like my own experienced when they arrived here in the United States were filled with acts of cultural humility from both sides. Those in the United States were willing to open even their own homes to families with whom they could not communicate. In many cases, a situation of mutual vulnerability existed as host families went out of their way to make the newly arrived feel as comfortable as possible as they navigated their unfamiliar surroundings.

I, too, came to the United States at an early age, so these were the welcoming stories I heard my parents reminisce about and how moved they were by such generosity, even when they did not know what such gestures meant at the time. Even when we settled into our own place, my father's coworkers would bring us our first Christmas tree and gifts so we could celebrate the holidays as the rest of those around us did. While these cultural exchanges were still one-directional, it did not necessarily include a domineering attitude that compelled one to embrace the other's traditions, nor were they provided out of pity—for they were truly acts of kindness based on my family's recounting of the initial encounter in this country. While some may have reached out to us because of the circumstances of our immigration experience—in particular, leaving an impoverished country—the cultural encounters that my family experienced were ones of comfort. If anything, it was the inability to understand one another linguistically that created the greatest barrier during these exchanges. Even with the lack of cultural understanding and the engagement of various differences in society as a whole during the seventies, the extension of hospitality allowed both sides to embrace a sense of humility and not humiliation that other encounters have demonstrated because of language, food, and other ethnic differences.

The opposite of cultural humility then—even when sometimes caused by ignorance—is humiliation when one party or the other feels inferior because of the dominance of the other. Often, newly arrived immigrants or minority groups tend to experience humiliation in a variety of ways; however, a dominant group can experience this as well due to a similar experience of being unable to navigate the encounters. A common experience for me and many other immigrants during the seventies and eighties occurred with food. At the time, the United States did not have the diversity of ethnic cuisines that exists today, and if some existed, these establishments were often relegated to certain districts, such as Chinatowns. In addition, fusion cuisine was basically unheard of during this time and so anything foreign definitely looked and smelled too exotic for most. In short, unknown tastes and smells tended to repel people rather than draw them together because of their unique taste and dining experience. I recall a time in high school when my mother made some traditional Korean dessert snacks out of mashed red beans that provided sweetness and texture. When a friend at school tried one, the immediate look on his face because of its unfamiliarity to his taste buds signaled a situation of humiliation. I remember discarding the rest of the snacks rather than sharing them with others because of his dislike for this new experience. Many immigrant children share such childhood memories, especially when their lunch boxes appeared and smelled foreign to those of their peers, which thereby created further isolation through such occasions of humiliation. Today, the opposite may be true as people desire such exotic dining experiences that differ from their everyday routine. However, the memories of my childhood experiences are filled with the ways our family differences allowed not for moments of humility for a true encounter of sharing one's background but, rather, for experiences of humiliation for being different in a new country.

Unfortunately, with any cultural encounter, experiences of both humility and humiliation are possible because our lives have shown that neither is truly absent in our personal experiences regardless of our ethnicity. Cultural encounters—whether based on geography or on generations—

*Preface*

invite both possibilities. In the case of intercultural marriages, these moments are always operative and may be more evident to those witnessing such unions than to the couples themselves who are living out this reality. It is through the sharing of these moments involving cultural acceptance ("humility") as well as cultural resignation ("humiliation") that we, the authors of this book, have been able to gather and organize the historical and contemporary experiences of individual couples so that others may also witness the changing landscape of our church and society. Indeed, intercultural union, with all its "rough edges," is layered in love and has always existed, but it continues to manifest in greater ways in our contemporary world—something that will only increase in intensity for future generations in our country and around the world.

Thus, we are attempting to capture voices ranging from an older couple to those of younger ones in order to expand the outlook of intercultural unions, as well as to enhance the marriage preparation period. This handbook is not a step-by-step manual for a successful marriage-prep program; rather, the intention of each chapter is to help us rethink our approaches in mentoring couples and to take culture seriously (not just as in ethnic or racial categories, but in the ways that we have all been formed). What you will find are theological questions and insights that allow you to glean pastoral approaches in your ministries to engaged couples.

The move from viewing marriage as the union of two persons—with each person inhabiting one bounded ethnic-cultural identity—to viewing marriage as a union of two persons, each of whom expresses a complexity of several sociocultural identity affiliations and accountabilities that continually interact with one another, mirrors, to some extent, the process through which official church teachings have approached culture, liturgy, and, by extension, the sacraments since the Second Vatican Council.

# Simon's Encounter of an Intercultural Union

Historically, Koreans have been much more opposed to marrying outside of their culture than is the case today. When we first arrived in the United States in the seventies, the idea of marrying someone who was not Korean was not culturally acceptable in the homeland or in the diaspora. The few "mixed marriages" that I encountered growing up usually involved

Korean wives who married U.S. GIs when they returned from service overseas on the Korean peninsula. In addition to many racial stereotypes about non-Koreans, the language barrier was the real challenge of embracing another culture since the English proficiency level of many Korean immigrants was nonexistent or very low at best. Thus, it was almost an unfathomable hurdle for non-Koreans to be received into larger Korean families, let alone into a faith community who only knew how to pray in their mother tongue. However, every now and then a brave soul would emerge in our ethnic faith communities.

I remember seeing non-Koreans at Mass and afterward, since going to church at a Korean Catholic Church meant spending the entire day there. Sundays were not only about the liturgical moment but also about the subsequent meals and various meetings, which seemed unending, especially to a child. It was during these long Sundays that I would see non-Korean husbands hanging around waiting for their Korean wives while they attended to all the activities of the day. I remembered them as being awkward—fish out of water—if not invisible as parishioners would stream by them, navigating the situation so as not to accidentally bump into them, which might cause a direct interaction. Obviously, these non-Korean husbands caught people's attention whenever they entered a room, for they were "different," even if they were often few in number (a couple at most) and no matter how hard they tried to blend into the walls so as to go unnoticed.

Growing up with this background actually made me appreciate the richness of diversity in intercultural unions today, but it was not without its challenges. Even though I spent all but two of my formative years in the United States, I still had a deep-rooted sense of cultural differences, especially on ethnic lines, because of this initial faith experience, which differed greatly from that of Ricky, the coauthor of this book. Isolation in both church and society created much of this attitude, which drew distinct lines between cultural groups in the United States, and only when it was necessary (such as at school) did we cross over. It would not be until I was ordained and started engaging various ministries in diverse parish communities that I came to understand the importance of such intercultural encounters for our church and society. It was also in my further doctoral studies along with my experience preparing couples for their lifelong journey together that I realized the complex dimension of cultural identity that went beyond ethnic lines and the necessity of forming such an identity in embracing our Catholic faith. Unlike Ricky, who experienced intercultural marriages at an early age and within his own family, my greater appreciation of such unions came as the next generation of Korean Americans began to engage in similar types of relationships and in greater numbers. Thus, the reflections of both our transformations in embracing an intercultural worldview are found throughout these chapters even though we have vastly different starting points when it comes to intercultural marriages.

# Ricky's Encounter of an Intercultural Union

I don't remember the exact moment when I was invited to serve as a ring bearer for the wedding of my aunt and uncle, Tita Barbara[1] and Uncle David, but at one point I found myself sitting at the dining room table surrounded by a room full of my Filipino relatives who were intent on teaching me the proper Western etiquette of fine dining. Apparently, in addition to serving as the ring bearer, I was expected to know these formal dining rules for the wedding reception. In hindsight that memorable lesson not only formally taught me Western etiquette in fine dining, but, more importantly, it also introduced me to the gift and complexity of intercultural marriages: Tita Barbara was Filipino American, and Uncle David was European American.

Naturally, terms such as *intercultural marriage* were not in my vocabulary, nor in my everyday experience. Up to that point, I only had known of Filipinos marrying other Filipinos. Furthermore, all of my neighbors in my suburban New Jersey neighborhood, the overwhelming majority of whom were Reformed Jews, were married to other Jewish spouses. Outside of one other family, we were the only Roman Catholic family in our neighborhood. In other words, based on my childhood cultural context, my interpretation of marriage was that people mostly married within their own ethnic cultural group. Thus, when I eventually met my future "Uncle David" for the first time, I was admittedly struck that such marriages were possible. I may have seen examples of intercultural couples on TV or even during our family ventures into New York City, but such experiences did not propel me to think more deeply about these relationships until I encountered an intercultural couple within my own family circle. In hindsight, my aunt and uncle introduced me to the concept that love transcends race, ethnicity, nationality, and culture, and for that I remain grateful to them.

Throughout the course of writing this book both Simon and I had opportunities to visit and interview four couples. These interviews confirmed what I already had known from previous ethnographic projects and my own academic interests: namely, the concept of culture is not a uniform nor a coherent concept, but a complex and dynamic construction, always transitioning and evolving. Growing up in Marlboro, New Jersey, my initial experience of distinguishing one cultural group from another was based not only on race (Asian Americans and European Americans) but also on other ethnic cultural distinctions, such as religion (Roman Catholic and Jewish). For our purposes, we can call this a *multicultural approach* to culture that *presumes* that people locate their own social cultural identity, more or less, within constructed boundaries *in relation to* other social cultural groups. However, what will become clear as we read through these pages is the simultaneous existence of interculturality: that is, all four couples that we interviewed expressed, claimed, or demonstrated various levels of micro- and macronegotiations of cultural values, meaningful practices, affiliations, and accountabilities. Thus, while acknowledging the existence of multicultural approaches to marriage, the goal of this book is to view and to approach more intentionally the sacrament of marriage through the lens of interculturality, as we believe that this particular lens has implications for theologians, pastoral leaders, and engaged and married couples today.

# Overview of the Book

On many levels, the intercultural process is evident throughout this book. For example, while we are articulating the developments and implications of the sacrament of marriage through the voices found in various cultures and the encounters between them, the organization and presentation of theological, pastoral, liturgical, and other perspectives are an intercultural task unto themselves. Without the latter, the former would be a compilation of interviews and observations left to the interpretation of the reader. Without the former, the latter would be a singular viewpoint or agenda from the authors themselves. However, by including the voices of intercultural couples along with the interchanges of the authors, what emerged in this work was the affirmation of the intercultural commitments of two theologians' approaches in witnessing the living out of the intercultural commitments of the couples. Readers will notice these two forms of interplay at work throughout the chapters.

Our ethnographic interviews with four couples of various ethnic and generational backgrounds reveal the emergence of cultural identities based on the social developments of U.S. society and the ecclesial advances since the Second Vatican Council. Chapter 1 interprets the council through monocultural, multicultural, and intercultural perspectives, thus setting the ecclesial context of this book. Chapter 2 provides a primer on intercultural marriage by providing a starting definition on the term *culture* and by introducing us to our first couple, Nina and Kevin Martin, both of whom are in their seventies. Their marriage took place around the time when the reforms of the Second Vatican Council were being implemented. Based on the interpretive data of interviews conducted by Ricky Manalo, the engagement period of Nina and Kevin reveal how couples often negotiate their own cultural identities between themselves and with other family members. Chapter 3 reflects the intercultural marriage preparation process based on actual engaged couples during the process of writing this book: Ella and Matthew were engaged in their fifties and Catherine and Peter in their twenties. Since marriage prep also needs to evolve from a monocultural to an intercultural process to keep pace with the realities of the lives of several engaged couples, this chapter provides insights that emerged from the ethnographic notes of Simon Kim, who identified these cultural realities for further reflection on the overall process. In chapter 4 we turn our attention to the liturgical celebration of the sacrament of marriage, specifically the Order of Celebrating Matrimony within Mass (hereafter OCM).[2] Here we present the insights that emerged from the ethnographic notes by Ricky Manalo, who interviewed our fourth married couple, Melissa Hoang and Roberto Gonzales, revealing what went behind the planning, preparation, and celebration of their wedding. Chapter 5 presents a theological reflection from a christological and pneumatological viewpoint to reveal the intentionality of Jesus's earthly mission and the ongoing Pentecost within the lived reality as church. Finally, we end this book with some concluding thoughts, mindful that the fruits of this book have implications for pastoral leaders, liturgists, and theologians who regularly prepare and reflect on the sacrament of marriage. It is important to remember that the presentation of these chapters emerged out of an intercultural process by listening to the voices in various intercultural situations. Future reflections of the church should continue this process of listening and challenging pastoral ministers to understand the deepening contexts of our lives, especially when they come together in such intimate ways.

Simon Kim and Ricky Manalo, CSP
Feast of St. Augustine of Hippo, 2020

# Acknowledgments

This project has indeed been an intercultural exercise from the beginning for all those involved. Not only did Simon and Ricky engage the theme of interculturality through ethnographic interviews of couples from various backgrounds and within different generations, but in the process of doing so quickly realized that another intercultural process was at work—one in need of further articulation of the intercultural exchange that was occurring between the two of them based on their upbringing, education, and current engagements. The former, based on research, included a straightforward approach of listening to a variety of stories of those already living out their intercultural unions or in the process of joining their lives in a similar way. Included in this listening was how the stories of their lives were being told as individuals and as couples within a singular narrative, for they were key in presenting their intercultural encounters in this book. The latter developed (and continues to develop) in the engagement of an external process as anyone undertaking a similar investigation will be quickly reminded of our own connections within this "web of interculturality." Through the emergence of this internal dynamic spurred by external events—an interchange between the experiences of the couples as well as the authors themselves—each chapter of this book underwent further refinement because of the interchange at work. Thus, what the authors found in writing each chapter was an ever-expanding exercise of interculturality and how this process is continually active on several levels.

As this web of cultural interactions and exchanges continued to expand, Simon and Ricky emphasized the two activities that were constants—the couples' lived experience of interculturality as well as the intercultural developments within the authors themselves through such invitations. Even though the two authors had many things in common (e.g., categorized as Asians, Roman Catholic, etc.), they still needed to negotiate their own cultural biases and a worldview that stem from such backgrounds. Not only were the authors "wedded" to the intercultural dynamics of this project—where paradigms were constantly being challenged, reevaluated, and reformulated through every encounter—but they were also "wedded" to each other's thought processes, especially when it came to strategizing on how best to present such a topic from the perspective of two celibate men. Thus, what emerged in these pages was quite different from the initial proposal. Both Simon and Ricky realized early that these revisions were necessary for an authentic representation of the sacrament of matrimony within an intercultural context, and that they could properly address the theme of interculturality only if they were receptive to being challenged in their approaches and open to repositioning them since such activities are constitutive aspects of an intercultural engagement. Thankfully, the publisher also understood the complexity of this project and had the patience to go along with the revisions that kept emerging. Simon and Ricky are especially grateful to Nancy de Flon at Paulist Press for also trusting in this process and in their abilities to accomplish this difficult, yet important work for both the Catholic Church and overall society.

Needless to say, these pages have undergone constant reworking that was initiated a couple of years ago when Simon[1] approached Ricky about this book project. Teaming up together seemed natural in the context of raising this important conversation since both of them have been calling for a greater emphasis on cultural competency in their own areas of expertise. It was from this original conversation that their theological reflections on the intercultural dynamics within the sacrament of matrimony would be further refined in every phone conversation, meeting in person, exchange of emails, and any other opportunity of engagement with each other.

Agreeing to collaborate on this project was the easy part for Simon and Ricky, but getting on the same page with one another in terms of timing and content was another story—one that also revealed an aspect of the intercultural process. Often, it seemed that when one author was ready, the other had commitments and vice versa. They quickly had to navigate their own pace of reflections, inquires, and the evolution of each other's thought processes, which at times seemed to coalesce into a unified consensus and at other times diverged. However, these challenges allowed both authors to realize an intercultural approach throughout each chapter of this book. For example, the initial proposal took a simpler approach to this project, highlighting the need for a better understanding of the sacrament of matrimony from a theological and liturgical perspective with an intercultural lens. This was a much simpler approach since it involved the authors' personal histories of intercultural engagements and their reflec-

*Acknowledgments*

tions as theologians and pastoral ministers in the church. However, as the project got underway, they realized that other voices needed to emerge as the "primary voices" and that the writers needed to fade into the background. Rather than detailing the intercultural dynamics in church and personal life through the lens of two unmarried men, Simon and Ricky deemed it necessary to allow the couples already involved in intercultural unions, or preparing for such, to speak to the intercultural encounters of our lives.

The interviews and conversations with those in the engagement period and at various moments of the couples' lives thereafter were not just evidence that affirmed the authors' position on this topic. Rather, the voices of those living out the daily challenges of cultural encounters in such intimate ways allowed Simon and Ricky to better articulate the church's teachings and liturgical practices within differing situations affecting the lives of those living them out daily. In doing so, the lived intercultural reality helps all of us to better illustrate the human and divine interchange found in God's revelation for every generation. Thus, bringing these voices to the forefront of this work was the intercultural dynamic that both authors understood as vital, but also needed to put into practice—knowledge and wisdom emerging from mutual partnerships where both sides are empowered to contribute and reflect upon the other in a similar manner to the respect wives and husbands have for each other. Therefore, we are deeply indebted to the couples who have participated in this project, for without them, we could not have engaged in our own process of such an intercultural reflection with our theological and ministerial backgrounds.

In addition to these couples of various backgrounds and generations, we are also grateful to Loyola Marymount University (LMU) and Brett Hoover who hosted an evening for us to present our initial thoughts. The conversation and feedback we received afterward provided the space for the authors to rethink their approaches in addition to the scope of their research. Though not radically different or opposed from their initial objectives, the LMU forum afforded both of them the chance to clarify the scope of the project along with the desired, yet reasonable outcomes.

# Chapter One

# Vatican II Milestone

## *From Monocultural to Multicultural to Intercultural*

REGARDLESS OF whether one views the Second Vatican Council (1962–65) as a retrieval of the past or an updating into the future, both perspectives would indeed consider this ecumenical council as a watershed moment in the history of the Roman Catholic Church. Undoubtedly, Vatican II propelled the church into the modern world through various reforms from liturgy to church structures to governance. The emphasis on the relational aspects of the faith—union with God and communion with the people of God—became the common theme to the changes affecting all areas of church life. Not only were foundational aspects such as the sacraments presented in this manner, but the idea that the Roman Catholic Church was now a global reality required that all cultures be acknowledged and respected. Thus, Vatican II gave special consideration to the care of individuals and their diverse backgrounds.

In the first document promulgated at Vatican II, the Constitution on the Sacred Liturgy (*Sacrosanctum Concilium*), the council leaders gave such considerations by addressing the need for liturgical adaptations in different parts of the world. "Even in the liturgy," they stated, "the Church has no wish to impose a rigid uniformity in matters which do not implicate the faith or the good of the whole community; rather does she respect and foster the genius and talents of the various races and peoples" (*SC* 37). By allowing the worship of the local people to develop within the Roman Rite, the council leaders called for a cultural accounting in the globalizing practice of the faith. While realizing the challenges and difficulties of this cultural exchange between people's lived experience and the liturgy itself, they still emphasized the importance of local contributions in worship by advocating that "an even more radical adaptation of the liturgy is needed" (*SC* 40) depending on the situation. Within this particular document, the movement from a monocultural expression of worship in liturgy was now moving into a multicultural realm of possibilities.

In doing so, conciliar debates had taken into account the people of God beyond Europe and North America. While addressing the growing diversity of the Catholic population throughout the world, these conciliar reflections still could not anticipate how human movement today would alter how people would congregate outside their places of origin. The diverse ways of worshiping in one's homeland as well as the emergence of adaptations in diasporic communities radically changed the council's initial notions of a world church—a worldwide community based on the increasing numbers of Catholics in different countries—to multicultural professions of faith in much greater proximity to the once seemingly monocultural or isolated neighborhoods. While Vatican II could not foresee the convergences of a world church in North America, Europe, or any other place in which the faithful pursued a better life for themselves and their families, the council's respect for individuals and cultural groups laid an important foundation for what was to come. The conciliar teachings are clear in that the church was moving beyond the confines of her previous historical realities and now had to embrace cultural encounters of the faith where the revelation of God would become much richer for the pilgrim people around the globe.

With such a perspective, the Second Vatican Council opened the Catholic faith to the world in a particular way. Once isolated in its own monocultural ecclesial culture, the council leaders propelled the church forward by acknowledging truths found outside the church walls—beyond the European or North American context—by recognizing the global developments of the Catholic faith. By doing so, the Catholic Church was now seen as a world church; however, the unity of faith across the globe did not necessarily warrant interaction among different cultural or ethnic groups. Rather, the acknowledgment of the growing diversity in the Catholic Church signaled a shift from monocultural to one that embraced a multicultural outlook.

For many, multiculturalism is a positive perspective, especially considering where the church was prior to Vatican II. The embrace of multiple expressions of the faith honored the cultural backgrounds of the faithful. However, multiculturalism has its limitations, too, as the acknowledgment of diversity also requires greater interaction among differing cultures, which multicultural outlooks did not necessarily require. What transpired in this country was the replacement of the European national parish with ethnic faith communities created by immigrants outside of Europe, even when they resided in the same parish boundaries. Often, this multicultural movement provided intercultural space for new immigrants to this country but did not consider their presence as constitutive in the cultural enhancement of the established churches and simply saw them as adding more numbers to the overall Catholic population.

But the reality of greater interaction between differing cultural groups also existed *between and among* the council members themselves during the sessions of Vatican II. To believe that more than three thousand cardinals, bishops, religious leaders, and theologians were rigidly uniform in their cultural worldviews is to live in an imaginary world. Melissa J. Wilde demonstrated how the interacting of four distinct cultural groups of bishops[1] led to the progressive outcome of the council, despite the institutional power base of conservative groups within the Vatican.[2] Intercultural strategies between these cultural groups centered around differing interpretations of church authority: progressives promoted collegiality while conservatives created a hierarchical organizational structure. In the end, the progressive groups "built a far more extensive and flexible organization than their conservative counterparts...[and thus] were more successful at developing compromise positions the vast majority of bishops could support."[3] In short, Vatican II may be viewed as an ecclesial gathering that took place in one geographic location and consisted of interacting and distinct cultural expressions of the one Roman Catholic faith.

Diversity regarding intercultural marriages has followed a similar trajectory. Many no longer have to cross their country's borders to find a diversity of cultures and peoples. Human migration, whether by force or by choice, has brought people together in ways unimaginable a generation or two before. Thus, the encountering of peoples from all over the world in the workplace, schools, parishes, and neighborhoods has afforded people greater opportunities for engagement in very personal ways. The encounter of those similar as well as different has created an acceptable environment in which cultures, races, generations, and so forth can be united in the sacrament of matrimony at an unprecedented rate. Not only is such acceptance found in the church, but current ecclesial reflections of such unions are in dialogue with the social and political movements of a specific locale as well.

# Intercultural Marriage

For example, for the U.S. church and society to reach acceptance of different ethnic groups coming together in marriage required two significant events. First, as noted above, the Second Vatican Council opened the doors of the church to the world, an opening to one that was both familiar and the unfamiliar to come. Second, the U.S. legal system had to amend restrictive laws to allow such intercultural marriages to occur. In 1967, *Loving v. Virginia* opened the way not only for Blacks and whites to join together in matrimony, but for any other ethnic groups to enjoy the blessings of creating a family in the midst of such cultural differences.

These cultural interactions are illustrated in the liturgy as called for by *Sacrosanctum Concilium*, especially in the marriage rites. The Order of Celebrating Matrimony further highlights these developments as revisions to the liturgical celebration initiated at Vatican II are continually at work even today as each version of the rite addresses the diversity and complexities of people's lives throughout the decades. When comparing the intentions of the Second Vatican Council found in the Roman Rite of Marriage in 1969 with the recent English translation of the Order of Celebrating Matrimony released in 2016, we find that the ceremony itself has remained relatively the same; however, the inclusion of certain cultural nuances in the latest ritual indicates that popular cultural devotions have become a part of the larger church's understanding of celebrating the union of two people. In particular, the recent inclusion of the *arras* and *lazo* along with the elimination of certain practices (such as unity candles) are indicative of cultural shifts in our liturgical approaches in which the faithful, regardless of past cultural understanding, are invited into the richness of these devotional ways of expressing one's love for each other, the wider community, and the Creator who binds us all together as one family.

Therefore, the 1969 version was a product of the renewal sought at Vatican II. The focus of the ritual at that time was to transmit the sacramental understanding of marriage as this became a constitutive part of the council's desire that the faithful have a full and active part in the prayers of the church. In order to do so, the couple would have to be better prepared in engaging the sacraments through better knowledge of what the church and civil authorities required of them.

In March 1969 the Congregation for Divine Worship issued a new Order for the Celebration of Marriage [*Ordo Celebrandi Matrimonium* (*editio typica*), Vatican Press, 1969]. It is a product of the liturgical reform initiated by the Second Vatican Council. The old rite as set forth in the Ritual and Missal was found in many respects to be inadequate. The *Constitution de Sacra Liturgia* (art. 77) laid down as a principle of reform: "The marriage rite now found in the Roman Ritual is to be revised and enriched in such a way that the grace of the sacrament is more clearly signified and the duties of the spouses taught."[4]

The first expectation of the church is easily understandable since couples were coming to the church to have their marriages blessed before the community. However, the second expectation is not always explicit but requires further investigation since the church's understanding of marriage developed as both an ecclesial and a civil matter. The new Order is not a "complete departure" but an evolution of existing customs as they pertain to "substance and structure of national and regional rituals." "The new Order is not intended to do away with existing customs but to provide the substance and structure of national and regional rituals. It is a '*ritual-type*' which may be freely adapted to meet cultural and pastoral needs."[5] Therefore, it is imperative to acknowledge that one of the English versions after the Second Vatican Council originated from the "Irish hierarchy" with a "distinctive character of its own."[6] Such a cultural viewpoint expressing the union between two peoples requires ongoing cultural developments to capture the reality of the richness and diversity of the couples today.

## Ongoing and Emerging Interculturality

While marriages have always been intercultural in the broadest sense, our inquiries and encounters further validate the need to highlight how today's unions are pressing the church to articulate the complexities of cultural encounters along with the gifts within each couple as intercultural marriages today are becoming more and more visible in our society. Previous "monolithic" notions of society, church, and the family, for example, did not simply disregard culture but, rather, assumed the other in the so-called melting pot schema. We now know that this type of mindset seemed plausible when differences originated from one continent alone, that of Europe. Biological similarities (being Caucasian, for example) helped further this

# Intercultural Marriage

approach that various differences could merge into some type of unified conglomeration.

Furthering this notion of church and society meshing into an American version of a singular communal reality was advanced with the U.S. influence throughout the world. The global embrace of Western ideals perpetuated by U.S. ideals of a democratic form of government and the capitalistic push for consumerism gave the impression that such commonalities based on development could cause all cultures to evolve to mirror one another. World developments over time have shown that this is not the case today; however, such notions based on both the self-proclamation and the exportation of one country's ideals made it seem possible in the past. Today, global developments highlight the fact that differences based on cultural backgrounds do not simply disappear or melt away into a singular ideal. Rather, increasing human movement around the world reveals the need to preserve one's cultural identity of the homeland while engaging others in diaspora. Thus, the need to understand one's past heritage to embrace new encounters with others is not an optional reality but one that needs to be acknowledged within the intercultural process.

While many avenues of engagement within an intercultural process may exist, the starting attitudes must be similar. Here we return to the notion of cultural humility and not humiliation as the attitude that must be held with those involved in such engagement. While a blank slate cannot exist in cultural exchanges, the dismissal of the other because of the foreignness to one's own experience or the longevity of one's cultural position in a certain place will always lead to some form of humiliation illustrated by the resignation of one's heritage. Cultural sensitivity means that the other is taken seriously even within these conditions.

Difficulties even with this approach of humility still exist, especially since the Catholic faith employs a "complex mechanism of recall, assumptions and associations of past events, specific interpretations and meanings which are distinct to this religion."[7] Such a "collective interpretation" naturally colors the intercultural engagement as the appearance of correctness—right or wrong or at least an appearance of a "better choice"—because of one's association with the Catholic faith. When such polarity exists, then what has traditionally happened in the past begins to emerge again. Previously, attitudes of superiority and correctness have led to one cultural perspective being brought to the other's situation, thereby supplanting one's "inferior" existence. Such approaches have been found to be problematic in the inculturation process where mutual respect (cultural humility) has been absent. Orlando Espín refers to a more mutual exchange as interdiscursive dialogue:

> What he/she understands and lives as truth; and I, within and from within my own cultural perspective, will contrast and perhaps assume that truth, because I have discovered it as truth (within and from within my cultural perspective), "witness" to the other, again in an open inter-discursive dialogue, what I have come to understand and live as truth, inviting the other to question and/or grow in what he/she understands and lives as truth—thereby moving the process into an ever-deepening and continuing dialogue where truth is discovered and affirmed, over and over, through mutual witnessing, contrasting dialogue, and non-colonizing reflection.[8]

There are two exchanges or encounters that we must consider when it comes to an intercultural perspective for our context regarding matrimony. First, since couples of various backgrounds are involved, there is an intercultural engagement between the couple as they present themselves to each other. Within this presentation are the cultural truths or heritage(s) held within each individual. The union of the two is to forge in a creative way, through interdiscursive dialogue, a new common understanding in reflecting on one's past to embrace the present realities in hopes of a future together.

> *Tradition, therefore, is not merely or mainly a recall of the past or a reference to it. Rather, it is the present interpretation of the past in reference to the future.* Present interests and hopes for the future drive and legitimate the complex web of recalls, assumptions and associations we call the past. Thus, the present projects a future that needs to be legitimated by a past that is, or so it seems, constructed by interpretations of and from the present's memory; and in doing this, the present "creates" a past which is then declared to be stable, self-evident, "objectively there," and ready to be mined for justifications for the present's legitimation needs.[9]

The second encounter involves the church, the priest or person preparing the couple as well as the liturgical celebration itself. In this encounter involving multiple parties, the tendency is to deposit the faith and other information regarding the requirements of the engagement period as well as the liturgical guidelines. This type of "banking model" arises from previous inculturation experiences in which the church or other so-called experts primarily in the Western industrialized world were seen as possessing greater or universal truths. Thus, this approach simply required the "depositing" of the faith or other worldly knowledge to those who were "less than"—less experienced, less mature, in lesser financial stability, and so forth—so that others could develop in a similar manner. This has typically been the case with the inculturation approach; however, inculturation may have other more positive facets if cultural humility and mutual respect are present. Because previous encounters of inculturation demonstrated a type of universal truth that others had to conform to even with cultural considerations, true interdiscursive dialogue did not emerge.

In this second encounter, couples have to engage church processes with specific parochial guidelines along with liturgical norms that can be used as a type of engagement in which couples must conform to certain beliefs and practices. This process, also known as "liturgical inculturation," will be explored in more detail in chapter 4. While not discounting the validity and usefulness of faith and cultural practices of the church, the understanding of their importance should arise out of an intercultural engagement, one that is interdiscursive. A primary difference between inculturation and intercultural engagement goes beyond just cultural sensitivity. What is allowed in the latter is a discussion that both compares and contrasts one's past to engage the present as well as looking to the future. The former presupposed a universal truth that had to be illustrated by the particular experiences of individuals and groups rather than allowing one's cultural diversity to allow a universal expression of people's lives. It is important for moments of awareness when individuals and couples come to understand for themselves the connection of their cultural lives with ecclesial culture.

Chapter Two

# In Good Times and in Bad

*Setting the Context for Intercultural Marriage*

*Ethnographic Notes by Ricky Manalo, CSP*

## Introduction

CHAPTER 1 offered an ecclesial overview of interculturality that emerged from Vatican II. Chapter 2 provides a primer on intercultural marriage to answer preliminary questions on culture and intercultural marriage and introduces us to our first married couple, Nina Chen and Kevin Martin. An intercultural lens then observes how our couple navigates through their engagement period, which occurred between 1973 and 1974. My ethnographic interviews with this couple also demonstrate how various cultural values, sensibilities, and accountabilities interact with one another as they prepared for their sacrament of marriage.

## Part One: A Primer on Intercultural Marriage

### WHAT IS CULTURE?

For the purposes of this book, we use the term *intercultural marriage* rather than *interethnic marriage*[1] since the term *culture* could be viewed as the values and meaning-making activities that individuals or groups *practice* in order to express, maintain, or negotiate the identity boundaries that resonate more readily within socially constructed groups. Culture involves not just *any* human practice, but practices upon which *meaning* is attached, however small in value or deep in significance. The term *practice* is taken from *practice theory*, which emerged from the writings of social theorists during the late 1970s. These theorists sought to explain the interplay between the routine activities we do each day, whether functional rituals such as housekeeping chores, or those that hold meaning in social and civic structures or religious institutions. These daily rituals, intentional or not, become ingrained through sheer repetition and serve to orient us in our world. Thus, cultural, artistic, musical, symbolic, and linguistic practices are able to express a person or a group's identity while simultaneously expressing their interpretation of the world in relation to other people. As such, a *cultural group* becomes composed of people who more or less share similar cultural identity practices. A cultural group can be based on race,[2] such as African Americans, Asian Americans, European Americans, or on ethnicity,[3] as with Hispanics, who encompass many countries of origin but have Spanish-speaking ancestry. Culture can also refer to people who share similar experiences of income, work, age, religion, gender, sexuality, or lifestyle. These can include groups known as middle class, poverty ridden, or blue collar; generational categories such as baby boomer or Generation X; and those defined by sexuality, such as the LGBTQ community. Since we may each affiliate with several social classifications, hold a specific country of origin, and live in a particular way, we inherently hold multiple cultural identities within us, before we even think to claim any named group we encounter. For example, I am a Filipino American, Roman Catholic ordained priest, male, from Generation X, and born in Brooklyn, New York. While I may not notice the micronuances of my identities, they are present within me and influence my view of the world. At the same time, I may at times negotiate the degree to which I participate in or feel accountable to each of the cultural groups that form my identity. For example, as I am a second-generation Filipino American, I continue to negotiate the degree to which I participate in and connect with the Filipino cultural traditions and practices that my parents have handed down to me. There are some Filipino values that I have embraced over the years, while there are others that I no longer value or practice in my everyday life. This accepting or discontinuing of inherited cultural daily practices, rituals, and traditions, like other societal and civic practices, changes throughout generations. This book intentionally focuses on "intercultural marriage," because we are specifically observing the interacting cultural identities that each person brings to their marriage, as distinct, but not unrelated to, dynamics of union identity, such as interfaith, interreligious, or interethnic marriages.

## WHAT IS INTERCULTURAL MARRIAGE?

Despite the overwhelming increase in intercultural marriages over the past few decades, few resources exist on this subject.[4] Some sources prefer to use the term *interethnic marriages*, while others, particularly in the arena of intercultural communication, use the term *intercultural marriages*. According to a 2015 Pew Research report, 17 percent or one in six United States newlyweds were married to someone from a different race or ethnicity. This is a fivefold increase from 1967, when it was noted to be only 3 percent.[5] Some key findings include the following:

- A growing share of adults say interracial marriage is generally a good thing for American society.
- Asian and Hispanic newlyweds are the most likely to be intermarried.
- The most common racial or ethnic pairing among 42 percent of newlywed intermarried couples includes one Hispanic and one white spouse.
- Newlywed Black men are twice as likely to intermarry into another culture as compared to newlywed Black women.
- An educational gap has begun to emerge in intermarriage, beginning in 1980.
- 14 percent or one in seven U.S. infants are multiracial or multiethnic persons.
- Honolulu has the highest share of intermarried newlyweds of any major metropolitan area in the United States.[6]

The Catholic Church considers the sacrament of marriage to be a covenantal relationship between spouses and God, as defined in *The Catechism of the Catholic Church*:

> The matrimonial covenant, by which a man and a woman establish between themselves a partnership of the whole of life, is by its nature ordered toward the good of the spouses and the procreation and education of offspring; this covenant between

baptized persons has been raised by Christ the Lord to the dignity of a sacrament. (*CCC* 1601)

In this context, intercultural marriage considers the *cultural interactions and dynamic processes* that occur between a husband and a wife before, during, and after the establishment of their matrimonial covenant between themselves and God. These intercultural dynamics include shared and contested value systems, varying understanding of meaning, and practices that point to or are expressive of "the good of the spouses and the procreation and education of offspring." As such, there is also a host of cultural interactions that occur throughout intentioned married couples, such as the family backgrounds of each of the spouses, degrees of accountability toward religious affiliation, ethnic and racial identities, and their social upbringing and classes. While *all* marriages are intercultural, whether couples share similar racial or ethnic backgrounds or not, every intercultural celebration of matrimony *culturally* expresses and points to the covenantal relationship between the husband and the wife, and between the couple and the triune God. Their whole relationship occurs within a particular local church community and is also part of the larger ecclesial universal church.

# Part Two: The Intercultural Engagement Period of Nina Chan and Kevin Martin

Having set a foundation for understanding intercultural marriage within a Roman Catholic context, it is time to introduce us to our first married couple, Nina Chan and Kevin Martin. Nina and Kevin met during a party in the spring of 1973, while they were both students at Rutgers University, New Brunswick, New Jersey. The couple married in the Cathedral Basilica of the Sacred Heart in Newark, New Jersey, on November 30, 1974. Nina and Kevin are part of the generation of people who were young adults during the time that immediately followed the conclusion of the Second Vatican Council. Nina was thirty years old and Kevin was thirty-one when they became engaged in 1973. The last session of the council occurred on December 8, 1965. Nina immigrated to the United States from the Philippines a year later, in March 1966. The revised *Rite of Marriage* was pronounced ready for use three years later, in March 1969. Four years afterward, Nina and Kevin met and became engaged and married in 1974. Their wedding brought together their religious and ethnic cultural backgrounds as well as their families, which also offered great reflection on how intercultural dynamics can form and inform relationships and marriage. Nina is a Filipina American who was born in the Philippines, baptized Roman Catholic as an infant, and grew up in a very large family of four sisters and three brothers. Nina was second to the youngest. Kevin, on the other hand, is European American and was born and raised in Montclair, New Jersey. He is the youngest of two sisters and two brothers and was baptized a Congregationalist Protestant.

A few months before my visit, I emailed Nina and Kevin a cultural identity inventory (see appendix A). The inventory lists eighteen "cultures and co-cultures."[7] During our second interview, I asked each of them to choose the top three cultures or closely related cultures with which they resonated the most during their engagement period. Kevin selected three cultures in the following order: (1) gender/sexual orientation, (2) education, and (3) social class. Nina, asking if she could choose four cultures, selected (1) religion, (2) race, (3) social class, and (4) education.

After spending some time discussing why Nina and Kevin chose their particular cultures, we noted the cultural groups or "cultural links" they shared in common and those "cultural distinctions" they did not share. The cultural links they shared were education and social class. The cultural distinctions they did not share were religion and race. Initially, it could appear that cultural links serve as natural connecting points for common interests of compatibility between couples. Nina and Kevin both went to college and obtained higher education degrees, so it would appear they valued the cultural link of education. Cultural distinctions or cultures they do not share could be presumed to be potential sources of tension and conflict. However, intercultural dynamics between engaged and married couples involve complex processes of negotiation. As a result, different and unexpected outcomes can emerge to reaffirm or contest preliminary cultural assumptions that couples have for one another. In turn, these can significantly change any preliminary assumptions between the couple that might seem obvious, due to cultural distinctions that are not mutually shared.

# CULTURAL LINKS: EDUCATION AND SOCIAL CLASS

Intercultural dynamics can provide helpful starting points for sharing and dialogue in a pastoral setting by utilizing available information for fuller conversation. It is important to then remain open to how each person interacts with the various cultural dynamics that unfold. In my conversation with Kevin, we began by talking about the cultural link of education, since Kevin had obtained an undergraduate degree from Carlton College in Minnesota and a master's degree in economics from Cornell University.

> Kevin: "I guess I was in the upper middle-class subculture there [in New Jersey] and particularly in my family subculture. Intellectual ability had a very high value placed on it."
>
> Ricky: "So education, that was really a value for you?"
>
> Kevin: "Yes, it was something that I thought...you're *really something* if you're smart. And I have to say, to some degree I passed that on to my kids."

Nina had an equal passion for education. She enrolled at Seton Hall University in Newark, New Jersey, for her first year of college and then transferred to Rutgers University, also in New Jersey. At one point during our interviews, she expressed some unease about her time at Seton Hall University. Through the course of conversation, it appeared that her unease was mostly due to her ethnic background and being the only Filipina woman in a classroom setting, where the majority of her classmates were men of European American ethnicity. There may have been other ethnic minorities present with her in class at the time, but during our interviews she was not able to recall other student ethnic backgrounds with any certainty.

> Nina: "At first I was afraid they might think [she laughs]...I didn't want them to think that Filipinos were dumb."

This particular disposition affected her study habits, as she noted:

> Nina: "I was just so...you know, so studious."

Social class was the second cultural link shared by both Kevin and Nina.

> Kevin: "Being in an upper-middle-class family...that was definitely a strong part of my culture....Your parents

> had gone through the depression, or came of age shortly after the depression during World War II perhaps....They got the Protestant work ethic and save, save, save and [then] you build a brick house and you move and forge ahead; you make a better life for yourself and your children and pass the economic status of your parents....Building your assets, financial security: I was very conscious of that. That certainly was a big part of my culture, and for better and for worse, still is."

Nina also resonated with the importance of social class, but her experience of being raised in the Philippines was different from Kevin's experience, which was influenced by his parent's work ethic. Nina's Filipina mother, Isabella, married a Chinese man, Peter Chan, who was born in the Fujian province of China. Peter was a highly successful businessman and the owner of an extremely lucrative coconut plantation in the Quezon province in the Philippines, the area where he and Isabella raised their family.

> Nina: "I was brought up with security, but not in a conscious way....We're all brought up in a certain class. It's almost like you don't marry below that. It's not conscious; it's just there....My parents did not indulge in conspicuous consumption, but I knew that we belonged to a certain class that [was] different from [others]."

While Nina and Kevin's cultural links of education and class served as entry points for sharing their stories, intercultural nuances and distinctions eventually came to light. Nina's experience as an immigrant while studying in Seton Hall University and her need to represent her Filipino heritage was different from Kevin's Protestant American lineage and work ethic that he inherited from his parents. Nina and Kevin's different cultural experiences led to different outcomes of how they lived their inherited cultural values of education and class. While cultural links can serve as seemingly similar starting points, interpretations of cultural values and how they are put into practice can become more complex. Thus, <u>care is needed so as not to presume any insights</u> when applying an intercultural context during marriage preparation or other pastoral discussions, since couples who share cultural links can apply these backgrounds and values very differently between themselves.

## CULTURAL DISTINCTIONS: RELIGION AND RACE

When Nina and Kevin shared stories of how they each viewed religion and race, intercultural dynamics immediately came to the fore. During our interviews, I admittedly presumed that Nina's Roman Catholic identity might clash with Kevin's Protestant identity during their engagement period, but again the dynamics of intercultural marriage relationships are not always predictable. I suggested their shared values of religion and race might serve as starting points for them to collectively understand Nina's approach to her Roman Catholic and Asian American identities, and Kevin's Protestant background and upbringing in mainstream North American culture.[8]

### *The Cultural Distinction of Religion*

Before my interviews with Nina and Kevin, I knew that each of them grew up in a different religious tradition and that together they formed an interfaith couple.[9] Their relationship echoed a 2015 report by the Pew Research Center that revealed interfaith marriages to be on the rise.[10] The same report compared recent and older marriages, where 39 percent or four in ten Americans who have married since 2010 or so with a spouse who is in a different religious group. Before 1960, the number of people in religious intermarriages was much lower at only 19 percent. Kevin was a baptized Protestant at the time he met Nina.

> Kevin: "When I was maybe twelve or so, my sister Joan went to a Billy Graham revival meeting, [which] had an impact on her, and I started going to a Baptist Church...[and they] kinda recruited me to be a good 'born againer.' And I started reading the Bible and what-not. But that [faded] a little bit."

He eventually became a "nominal Protestant" (his term) due to an incident when the minister neglected to write a letter of recommendation for his sister, Joan. After he met Nina, however, the role of religion once again became more significant:

> Kevin: "At the time of my marriage, I needed to switch to Catholicism because I wanted to get married. But I figured I could be a nominal Catholic as a nominal Protestant. I certainly saw myself as a nominal Protestant. I wasn't a very spiritual person in those days. I did appreciate the spirituality with which Nina practiced her religion."

A week before their wedding, Nina and Kevin met with Fr. Mark, a priest at Sacred Heart Cathedral, whom Nina had "selected" (her term) to preside at their wedding. I was surprised to learn that this one-time meeting was the extent of their marriage preparation, presumably because Kevin was living in Los Angeles and too far away to attend regular sessions with the pastor. Yet, neither of them attended any premarital seminars or took any premarital inventory, which are current-day common requirements. During that meeting, Kevin's admiration for Nina's spirituality became central to their conversation:

> Kevin: "Fr. Mark was very flexible. He just sat down with me and we talked one-on-one for a while about what my religious background was and I totally won him over when I said, 'Well, I see the way Nina practices her religion and it's so enjoyable to her...that seems to me the way that religion should be.' So [Fr. Mark] thought, 'Okay, this guy is not too bad, we could live with this [laugh].'"

Roman Catholicism was an important part of Nina's daily life, because she had grown up in the Philippines where the majority of people are Roman Catholic.[11]

> Nina: "I went to Catholic high school [and during my] sophomore [year], it suddenly dawned on me that without God, life has no meaning...that God is the one that gives meaning to life. I was so sure. That's when I started to go to—in the summer, there's a seminary

> nearby, a teaching church, a hundred or more seminarians—I started to go to the weekday Mass. It was so beautiful!"

Ricky: "So at the time of your wedding, it was obviously important for you. Would you have married outside of the church?"

Nina: "I would *not* have married outside the Catholic Church. Because it's important to me that I'd be married in the church. Outside of the church? I could not do that. It would have to be by a priest."

Ricky: "So for both of you: Do you remember when you began to talk about religion? What was that conversation like?"

Nina: "I didn't really ask him to convert. He offered...."

Kevin suddenly interrupted in disagreement.

Kevin: "Well, no, you didn't *ask* me to convert, you just said, 'We ain't getting married, if you don't [laugh]!'"

Ricky: "So was it implied or was it explicit?"

Kevin: "I don't remember exactly. I was pretty sure in my mind that I would need to convert."

Nina: "Oh, I remember with Fr. Mark...he said if he doesn't convert, we would have to be married in the chapel, instead of the main church....I started, like, crying....I felt like an outcast. [To Kevin] But I don't remember asking you to convert, so maybe you saw that....You knew I was very religious at the time. You were very aware of it...."

Kevin: "Oh yeah, religion wasn't any big deal for me to convert to Catholicism. I was a nominal Protestant anyway."

## *The Cultural Distinction of Race and Nationality*

Nina had mentioned that she felt a responsibility to represent all Filipinos "in a good light" (her words) when she was a student at Seton Hall University. However, both Nina and Kevin agreed that they have also felt a form of racism with Kevin's mother, when Nina visited Kevin's parents in North Carolina. Kevin's mother, Joanne, invited Nina to an event at a local country club, where at one point Joanne met an acquaintance and introduced Nina as just "Nina," rather than adding the descriptor of "her daughter-in-law."

Kevin: "My memory was that [my mother] didn't introduce [Nina] as her *daughter-in-law*. And I think it's because she thought that the person to whom she was introducing Nina might've been prejudiced. So [my mother] was conscious of the fact that Nina was of a different ethnicity, the darker skin color...[as if] she was trying to protect her own social status....That was the only time I encountered that. I always warned Nina about my mother. My mother was very good in socializing; always left a very good impression."

Nina: "I always liked his mom, [but] that was a shock to me when she took me to that country club, [and said] 'This is Nina' and not adding 'my daughter-in-law.' And so when I told it to Kevin that night he was so angry. I was offended, but I wasn't going to let it bother me. But he said, 'I had always told you that my mother was a hypocrite. Now do you believe me? My father would not have done that to you.'"

While Nina and Kevin's intercultural differences had emerged around their cultural links of education and class, their concern about race became a shared point of meeting rather than contention. In short, Nina's hurtful encounter with racism brought them closer together. This circumstance illustrates how intercultural marriage dynamics can influence the outcome of couples who may not share cultural links at the start of their relationship but realize an unexpected opposite outcome when confronted with an unforeseen situation.

## *The Cultural Distinction of Family: Individualism-Collectivism in Intercultural Marriage*

While neither of them chose family as one of their "top three" cocultures, this theme came up quite frequently as it related to familial accountability and individual choices, apart from familial traditions. Intercultural theorists label this spectrum between family obligation and individual choice as the individualism-collectivism cultural value. According to leading intercultural theorist Susan Ting-Toomey, the cultural value spectrum of individualism-collectivism is the most significant distinction found among all cultural groups.

> Basically, *individualism* refers to the broad value tendencies of a culture in emphasizing the importance of individual identity over group identity, individual rights over group rights, and individual needs over group needs. Individualism promotes self-efficient, individual responsibilities, and personal autonomy. In contrast, *collectivism* refers to the broad value tendencies of a culture in emphasizing the importance of the "we" identity over the "I" identity, group rights over individual rights, and in group-oriented needs over individual wants and desires. Collectivism promotes relational interdependence, in-group harmony, and in-group collaborative spirit.[12]

This cultural value spectrum emerged in my conversation with Kevin, when I asked him how much weight he gave to his family's influence when he was deciding whether to marry Nina. He responded,

> "It was always *my choice*, that whatever [my choice] was, you weren't going to quibble about it. They were either going to be supportive [of this choice] or not... and they were."

This is not to suggest that Kevin had no level of accountability toward or no degree of concern for his family. In another interview, when reflecting on his mother's reaction to his marrying Nina, Kevin shared,

> Kevin: "I'm sure [my mother] had some feelings when I told her that I was converting to the Catholic Church so we can get married...and I can't blame her for that."

But in the end, Kevin clearly expressed his attitude toward his family's approval of him marrying a Catholic as he smiled and said, "I have that same attitude: 'Fine, and if you disapprove, you don't have to come [to the wedding].'"

## *In Good Times and in Bad*

For Nina, however, her desire to seek approval was quite strong and came with a greater degree of accountability and obligation toward her family members.

Nina: "In a Filipino family, everybody has to have a say [laugh]. Even if it's just a comment....If someone gets married, you can say whatever. You have your opinion and it's okay to express it. So I wasn't surprised with Jacqueline [Nina's older sister]. [She] was like my Mom here [in the United States]. I always considered her my 'second mom' or 'my mom when I came to the U.S.' And she had the right to say anything and it wasn't offensive to me. It's out of love, it's not like... she feels responsible, both of them: Kuya[13] Dading [Jacqueline's husband; Nina's brother-in-law], both of them. They were brought up in that culture. They felt responsible for me. They're just being protective. It's nothing, and...that's how I took it, because that's the way it is to be taken, because that's really where they're coming from."

Kevin continued Nina's narrative as he described some of the cultural roots of his own independency:

Kevin: "Particularly American more so than European: going out to the frontier! And that was the thing in our American history...[even] if they did have with a family, they would just go West!"

Nina then continued her thought:

Nina: "...not just to the family, but to the nation, to the people: the Philippines. Just like when I went to school. I got straight As in Seton Hall, because I didn't want them to think Filipinos were dumb. So it was a very nationalistic way of thinking. It's not that my family didn't care."

Intercultural Marriage

# Correlations and Reflection

This chapter sought to provide a primer on intercultural marriage through the lens of an ethnographic interview project that involved a married couple who became engaged in 1973. The goal was *not* to present a comprehensive examination of intercultural marriage, since such an endeavor would have needed to include a larger pool of married couples and accompanying data. Rather, the authors believe that correlations between this chapter and the other chapters of this book have implications for theological reflection as well as potential insights for pastoral leaders who serve in the sacramental preparation and celebration of matrimony.

As a result of my interviews with Nina and Kevin, some correlations and reflective points can be drawn:

1. Locate the cultural identities and histories of all participants.
2. Narrative tools can be used to promote intercultural dialogue.
3. Develop skills for intercultural competence.

## 1. LOCATE THE CULTURAL IDENTITIES AND HISTORIES OF ALL PARTICIPANTS

Early on in my interviews with Nina and Kevin, there was a need for us to reflect on the meaning of culture and how we viewed ourselves as cultural persons. Intercultural relationships start with the presumption that all people regularly engage in forms of meaning making and practices that are expressive of particular worldviews and values. Usually, these cultural realms stem from perceived distinctions from other cultural groups or social systems. Throughout the interviews, Nina and Kevin were invited to share the cultural narratives that occurred during their engagement period. As the interviews progressed, other cultural identities and locations became pertinent, including friends and family members, as well as my own cultural location and disposition, since I was the person conducting the interviews. Therefore, the set of questions I presented, with this book in mind, and the choices I made to use particular tools, such as the cultural identity inventory, all affected the outcome of these interviews.

Consequently, pastoral leaders need to be aware of the various cultural dynamics and identities that are operative during the process of marriage preparation and sacramental celebration. As an official rite of the Roman Catholic Church, the sacrament of marriage has its history and cultural heritage.[14] This history continually interacts with the present and the cultural identities of couples, as well as the pastoral leaders who prepare them for marriage. Intercultural threads are woven into every present-day marriage preparation and celebration and can include the following: (1) the cultural identities that are represented separately and collectively by the husband and wife, whom they envision to be "one couple," as well as the cultural practices that might emerge as a result of their marriage; (2) the cultural locations of the official church as represented by the official teachings, histories, traditions, and doctrines on the sacrament of marriage; and (3) the cultural identities of the church representatives, such as pastoral leaders, clergy, and laypersons who participate in the ceremony and guide the intercultural process to prepare engaged couples for marriage.

## 2. NARRATIVE TOOLS CAN BE USED TO PROMOTE INTERCULTURAL DIALOGUE

When I began my ethnographic interviews with Nina and Kevin, my overriding methodology was grounded in the sharing of stories and the construction of narratives to discover the intercultural dynamics and nuances of all those involved in their wedding ceremony. This included Nina, Kevin, pastoral leaders, friends, and family members. The tools I employed, particularly the cultural identity inventory, were a starting point to prompt them to share their stories, faith beliefs, and cultural identity narratives.

As they share their stories, engaged couples, along with pastoral leaders, negotiate the boundaries that have defined their cultural identities. As John P. Bartkowski writes,

> I begin with the premise that narratives are "storied" in two senses. First, narratives are vital for organizing everyday experiences and imbuing life with meaning. Narratives enable storytellers to convey important cultural cues about who they are and who they are not, and to explain why certain courses of action are taken while others are averted....Other narratives draw on the logic of distinction and thereby underscore boundaries between different types of people and experiences.

Thus, some narratives employ bridging discourse, while others reflect boundary work.[15]

Layers of meanings eventually emerged that either competed with or complemented one another: "Thus, while narratives are an attempt to impose meaning and order on complicated experiences, they are ineluctably marked by contradictions, tensions, and ironies." As we shared our stories and conversation, Nina, Kevin, and I set boundaries that helped form the dynamics of cultural links and distinctions.

The sacrament of marriage is not just a joining together of two people, but a weaving of past and present cultural narratives and strands of history and lives that have been shared for generations. The use and proclamation of Sacred Scripture recalls the collective memory of the church as the particular words and prayer texts of the wedding rite, with its ritual, presidential prayers, words of consent, the blessing and giving of rings, and the nuptial blessing continue the biblical narratives and tradition that are now present in the love that the wife, husband, and couple share with one another, God, and our whole faith community.

## 3. DEVELOP SKILLS FOR INTERCULTURAL COMPETENCE

After Nina and Kevin selected their cultural and cocultural values, I proposed starting points for conversations to identify their cultural similarity, congruency, and cultural differences or distinctions. These starting points were to become a bridge to more in-depth intercultural conversations, with the intention of observing nuances and intercultural complexities that might emerge.

While the OCM represents a sacramental, ritual, and official gathering that brings together a host of cultural dynamics, their ongoing interweaving continues in the daily lives of the couple, long after the ceremony has ended. The consent given by the couple embodies this future reality:

- I, *N.*, take you, *N.*, to be my wife/husband. I promise to be faithful to you, in good times and in bad, in sickness and in health, to love you and to honor you *all the days of my life.*[16]
- Alternative form: I, *N.*, take you, *N.*, for my lawful wife/husband, to have and to hold, *from this day forward,* for

better, for worse, for richer, for poorer, in sickness and in health, to love and to cherish *until death do us part*.

One prominent question remains: How will the intercultural strands of Nina and Kevin's Christian faith and their accountabilities to cultural groups deepen, interweave, overlap, and harmonize all the days of their lives, until death do them part? Or will these strands somehow separate from one another? "For God, who has called the couple to Marriage, continues to call them to Marriage."[17]

Intercultural marriage is an ongoing and lifelong process of growth and part of the necessary development of intercultural capacity between spouses. In the guidelines *Building Intercultural Competence for Ministers* (BICM), the United States Conference of Catholic Bishops (USCCB) defines *intercultural competence* as "the capacity to communicate, relate, and work across cultural boundaries." While these guidelines were created for pastoral ministers, intercultural competence skills are indispensable for every married couple and can be divided into three areas: *knowledge*, *skills*, and *attitudes*.

- Knowledge of more than one perspective in any situation
- Knowledge of different interpretations of the same cultural reality
- Knowledge of the general dynamics of intercultural communication
- Knowledge beyond our first language

Skills entail the following:

- Ability to empathize
- Ability to tolerate ambiguity
- Ability to adapt communication and behavior

Attitudes include the following:

- Openness to others and other cultures
- A desire to learn and engage with other cultures
- Understanding intercultural interaction as a way of life, not a problem to be solved

- Mindfulness that there is always more to learn about our own histories, habits, and cultures and those with whom we share this world and matrimony[18]

Resources such as BICM are one among many other resources that couples and pastoral leaders can draw upon in order to ensure continued growth and development of intercultural skills.[19]

# Conclusion

Chapter 2 served as a primer to provide understanding of preliminary starting points for intercultural marriage and to introduce our first married couple, Nina Chan and Kevin Martin. My ethnographic interviews with this couple offered insight into how they interconnect the various cultural identity threads they held *before* the wedding ceremony. However, during their engagement period between 1973 and 1974, they did not participate in marriage preparation between them and the pastoral leaders of the parish, since no such preparation program was offered by their parish, beyond their one-time meeting with the parish pastor, Fr. Mark. Today most parishes offer more extensive marriage preparation processes that are conducted by both clergy and lay leaders at parish and diocesan levels. In chapter 3, we will explore the process of intercultural marriage preparation that takes place today as we continue the quest to develop better pastoral responses to this sacrament.

# Chapter Three

# For Richer or for Poorer

## *Pastoral Approaches for Preparing Engaged Couples*

### *Ethnographic Notes by Simon C. Kim*

THIS CHAPTER begins with a rationale for the need for the continual development of marriage preparation programs, especially in light of the changing demographics of today's church. While various approaches or methods have been employed, we are not attempting to present a "bible" on preparing intercultural couples by simply compiling best practices. Rather, all marriage preparation programs have their benefits; thus, it is our hope that this chapter helps widen the church's perspectives in preparing all couples. Throughout this chapter, a few practical applications along with actual couples' responses are included to demonstrate the intercultural aspects of such preparation.

## Introduction

In any uncharted waters, people venturing into new areas of the world quickly realize that certain skill sets are required for such a journey. Cartographers in the past drew upon available resources—both in their own personal expeditions of sailing up and down the seacoasts (repetition) as well as from the wisdom gained through the expertise of others (recommendations)—in order to accurately depict their knowledge of the places and how to navigate them. History has shown that such depictions have been both remarkably accurate given the limited tools accessible to each generation, as well as sometimes being wildly farfetched illustrations given their presuppositions, such as the world being flat. However, through the journeying of successive generations, such mapping and navigating of the open waters has been refined to the point where now we have accurate depictions based on satellite images of the land as well as GPS coordinates of where we are actually standing.

Marriage preparation programs in the Catholic Church have taken a similar trajectory, especially within the U.S. context. The European immigrant experience of congregating in ethnic enclaves in urban areas upon arrival and then moving out to suburban neighborhoods through successive generations provides this country's first context of intercultural expressions of marital unions. Physical movement away from the old country resulted in European immigrants embracing the different ideals of the host country while retaining some of the characteristics of the homeland. They used what was familiar to them back home to understand their place in a foreign situation. Thus, immigrants utilized some of the historic understanding of their rich heritage to re-create structures that retained their identity away from their homeland. Through this dynamic mapping of the old onto the new, navigating their own location in the midst of other neighborhoods became a necessary endeavor for the initial generations within this urban context. Marriages in this setting followed a similar pattern as couples, either immigrants or the offspring of immigrants, relied on models of what they had already witnessed as they navigated the new environments.

Another relocation, the physical movement away from urban ethnic neighborhoods into the suburbs, especially after the Second World War when the soldiers returned home and could relocate through government assistance programs, created a challenging new environment for many descendants of European immigrants. Relocating to suburban neighborhoods meant acquiring new neighbors comprising different European backgrounds and identities. The coming together of European descendants was not always "new" since some had crossed ethnic borders in urban communities previously. These courageous acts went against social norms and customs but were also so because of the many unknowns of such encounters. However, the new suburban setting with blurred ethnic lines allowed for intercultural marriages to become more commonplace—something that we take for granted and have become more accustomed to today. As descendants of Polish, Irish, Italian, German, and other immigrants from Europe started families with one another, these intercultural unions impelled couples to newly map their lives and navigate their differences in ways that were not prevalent in isolated urban communities. Not all was lost in these new unions, however, as certain cultural values and practices were retained and appropriated in people's lives when they caused little conflict. For example, Catholics professing an Italian heritage in Chicago still go back today to their "original" home church (now occupied by Chinese Catholics) on special feast days, preserving their traditions by carrying a statue of their patron saint through the neighborhood as their forebears once did.

Thus, the suburban church became an intercultural church through the resettlement of different European ethnic groups within the same neighborhood as well as through mixed marriages (culturally and between generations as well). Naturally, the suburban church became its own culture—a conglomeration of European devotions and expressions that has today become the so-called mainstream church we take for granted. What emerged from this was a seemingly monocultural worshiping environment seen as universal rather than the coming together of particulars. Such implications are still not fully understood, as similar processes occur today as diverse groups tend to follow a similar trajectory without considering the contribution that each particular culture is able to make to both church and society. However, if we are able to see this period of our social and ecclesial history as an intercultural convergence—where particular traits benefit the overall church and society—then we become more mindful of promoting an approach to diversity that is respectful.

A particular lesson among many that can be gained from this experience in regard to marriage preparation is that it takes time and conscientious effort to prepare couples carefully today because of the shifting demographics and context of people's lives. The complexity of the landscape for couples today due to the ongoing convergence of social and cultural factors cannot be immediately understood even with the church's two thousand years of tradition. New eras such as ones inaugurated by intercultural unions are part of the ongoing Pentecost, the coming together of God's people from different parts of the world, and today's version reflects this in a greater way than any other period in our church's history because of global human movement.

While immediate challenges and opportunities can sometimes be foreseen concerning such diverse unions, deeper underlying issues cannot always be grasped because they must be first lived out by the couples themselves. In other words, just as the sacrament of matrimony is not a singular event at the wedding ceremony but is rather the continual living out in the journeying of the two, intercultural mapping and navigation requires this as well. Often in marriage preparation, what is passed on to the new couples are the road maps and navigational know-hows of the previous generation, and rightfully so. Therefore, the wisdom from the actual lived experience provides an important aspect of the marriage preparation process. Included in this is also the wisdom gained by the clergy through their experience of accompanying people through difficult situations. However, today's couples of such differing backgrounds also require the time to understand their own situations that will continually emerge from their lives together. They will have to navigate the waters of marital unions of intercultural couples by being faithful to past traditions of their families and their faith, while at the same time patiently and painstakingly uncovering the new terrain for themselves as well as for both church and society.

Our past experiences allow us to anticipate some of the challenges, because what emerged from the suburban convergence are marriage programs that addressed the mapping and navigating necessary for couples where a new sociocultural neighborhood intermingled with their diverse ethnic backgrounds, albeit mostly a European American context of Catholicism. In the previous chapter we focused on Nina and Kevin's own intercultural process of dialogue as they reflected on their engagement period forty-five years earlier, and we employed some tools from the discipline of intercultural communication. While such communication skills are useful, an important consideration in preparing couples for matrimony is not necessarily just about gaining communication skills or managing conflict resolution because of our differences. Noted marriage expert John Gottman dispels these ideas:

> Perhaps the biggest myth of all is that communication—and more specifically, learning to resolve your conflicts—is the royal road to romance and an enduring, happy marriage.... The notion that you can save your relationship just by learning to communicate more sensitively [active listening] is probably the most widely held misconception about happy marriages—but it's hardly the only one.[1]

Communication and conflict resolution are still important, but they are not the "cure-all" to relationships.[2] Therefore, the starting point of marriage preparation is the individual's identity, which includes a cultural understanding of herself or himself since communication, conflict resolution, and other necessary skills for any relationships are held within a specific cultural context. The emphasis on culture within the marriage preparation process seeks to help the couples with their mapping and navigational skills especially within an intercultural context—providing the space for such communication and conflict resolution to have its proper place. While Gottman does not refer to intercultural mapping per se, I recently received an email from the Gottman Institute about the importance of "giving a story," which closely aligned with the narrative devices that were employed in chapter 2. In this email blast, the idea of sharing one's story is about tapping into one's cultural background. Contained in the email is the following:

> Ask your partner a question that allows them to share a story or memory. How did you celebrate the holidays when you were growing up? What is the best gift you've ever received? What are your favorite traditions or rituals around this time of year? What rituals would you like us to create and share together? Stories can be sweet, sad, sentimental, funny, or even painful—but they're always meaningful. Take the time to share a story and listen to your partner as they share theirs. Reflect on how your partner's story might have influenced how they see the world now.[3]

This emphasis on "giving a story" is about communication, which Gottman seems to dismiss earlier; however, upon closer examination, communication is still a valuable asset if it is understood in its rightful cultural context. Listening and support between the couples, then, is the resulting activity of the intercultural process within a marriage preparation. "In the strongest marriages, husband and wife share a deep sense of meaning. They don't just 'get along'—they also support each other's hopes and aspirations and build a sense of purpose into their lives together."[4] In short, these "hopes and aspirations" can be told only within their cultural setting and properly understood in the intercultural exchange between the couple.

Today's models or programs for marriage preparation were initiated in the late 1960s due to the changing landscape and the spark of renewal through the Second Vatican Council in which more attention was now paid to the laity. Marriage Encounter, which began in the late 1960s,

Engaged Encounter in the mid-1970s, and Pre-Cana with its FOCCUS inventory in the mid-1980s are the most common ones that dealt with specific issues of the pre- and postwedding situations arising from this suburban experience for the church. While these programs have adapted over the years by considering generational differences, they still rely on models or patterns studied during the initial intercultural convergence of people's lives in mostly the context of suburbia. As the church accompanies the changing landscape of neighborhoods once again, marriage preparation looks to models and programs of what has been discerned necessary and beneficial in the past, while at the same time it accompanies the couples with diverse backgrounds in order to better understand and to learn from this emerging context, which is becoming ever more common. Today new programs, such as Witness to Love, are emerging as a response to the need for renewed evangelization in marriage preparation as well as an acknowledgment of some of the complexities of contemporary society. Thus, what is symbolized in the exchange of vows before the church's minister is not a moment in time but a lifelong journey for both the couple and the church.

Just as the couple is on a lifelong journey with each other and with the church, the church in turn accompanies them in a reciprocal manner. The couple learns from each other and, in this exchange, mapping occurs. The church's engagement with this couple also allows the church to learn about the intercultural situation and how best to walk with them. The previous notion, especially in regard to the sacraments, was that the church's ministers had the answers or the road map to present to those before the church. As Vatican II reminded us, the church must learn from life in all sectors of society. Therefore, the church's accompaniment of the couple is an opportunity to deepen her understanding of cultural realities and the challenges that these intercultural encounters present to all of us. These challenges are, in fact, opportunities to deepen the deposit of faith of the Catholic Church. These ongoing social engagements and developments point to the diversity of creation God intended with humanity.

Marriage preparation with such an understanding requires the church's minister to be in a position of learning and growing just as the couples themselves are. At times, the church's minister may have a certain vantage point with experience and wisdom over young couples. However, the landscape of society is rapidly evolving, especially with the shifting demographics due to human movement (from state to state as well as country to country). Therefore, a humble posture is necessary in learning the cultural nuances of the couple and the emerging realities from such intercultural unions. This posture of humility allows for the journey of accompaniment to begin.

In the marriage ceremony, the representative of the church witnesses the sacrament being exchanged between the couple. This relational space into which the clergy is invited is a place of honor—an invitation into a "trinity" of relationships in the midst of the couple's lives. Thus, the marriage preparation is the beginning of such encounters for the clergy with the man, the woman, and together as a couple. The goal of the "six months"—the minimum period that couples are asked to reflect and prepare themselves—is more than a waiting period to ensure that they are ready for such commitments. It is more than just gaining knowledge about each other, the situations they may encounter when living together, the teachings of the church, and so forth. More importantly, this time of preparation is a gift where the priest or deacon already begins witnessing the growth of the couple's commitment to each other and to the church. As the couple grows closer to each other in this process, the priest or deacon deepens his relationship with them as well. Just as a successful marriage preparation reflects growth from wherever the couples find themselves, the deepening of the relationship with the clergy, the representative of the whole Body of Christ, is also an important reflection of the overall process.

As I have been blessed to encounter couples throughout my own ministry, I find that the fruits of such preparation continue to blossom beyond the wedding date. Couples return to the church, requesting a further deepening of their commitment to each other and the faith community by continually inviting the church into their ongoing celebrations of life as well as in moments of sorrow, especially in the death of a loved one. The relationship created in the marriage process for the couple with the church and the church's representative continues beyond the wedding date, as it ideally should.

There is no secret recipe, as any relationship takes time, effort, and compassion, especially because every individual is on their own personal journey and at a unique stage in their own lives—and this is a normal source of challenges for the couples. Therefore, it is important to encounter the couple in various settings beyond their visits to the parish office for meetings with church representatives, and beyond Sunday liturgies. Often, when younger couples are in this engagement process, I ask them to be involved in a ministry that will benefit both the couple and the community. This specific invitation deepens the "trinitarian" encounters, since different settings reinforce the relational efforts being taught in premarital workshops, weekend retreats, and so forth, and allows the Body of Christ to share in the couple's journey as well. Their involvement in the wider community is an integral part of any preparation as couples are given the opportunity to navigate their lives within this broader setting. The couple should be given the opportunity to put into practice the skill sets gleaned over the preparation period, first in safe environments within a loving company, so that they can gain the confidence to continue navigating uncharted areas of their own. Teaching couples to learn to map their lives within a faith community, in turn, is also teaching them to learn how to map their lives with the diversity of backgrounds they bring to their marriages.

The need for such mapping tools today arises from the fact that very few models, images, and so forth are available for couples entering into an intercultural union. While many can look to their own families, especially their parents, for clues on how to navigate this new stage of their lives, intercultural couples are also pioneers paving a new life together that will manifest their own upbringing, heritage, and current society; however, such encounters between worlds that are vastly different because of cultural, ethnic, and general differences, to say the least, also force couples to tackle unforeseen challenges. Such encounters can be both a blessing and traumatic at the same time. In the marriage preparation process, couples are being empowered to create new models of God's love for us and how to love each other with a breadth of diversity with which creation has presented us. Our successes today in preparing and empowering these encounters set the stage for future generations as this intercultural world will only present more such opportunities along with all its challenges.

Again, this is not to say that this work has not been done in the past. While intercultural relationships have been part of our modern church, the sheer number, from all areas of the world, is unprecedented because of the human movement that has happened and is still occurring in all parts of the world. In the past, some of these cultural and ethnic differences were addressed in the European immigrant population as subsequent generations blended together. In particular, when Catholics married non-Catholics, such differences were highlighted with few options presented. Often, a multicultural-interfaith approach was taken where people's lives were compartmentalized to preserve a "Catholic identity," especially when it came to their children. Today's intercultural unions cannot segregate but must come together not only in the individual's faith journey, but also with all the rich heritage one has been blessed with. An intercultural union is to reflect upon the richness and diversity that is found in our trinitarian experience of the church. The later chapter on why the intercultural encounter was highlighted in the life of Jesus and in the outpouring of the Holy Spirit speaks to God the Father's revelation to all sons and daughters.

# Mapping and Navigating Our Lives— Separately and Together

During the first encounter with an engaged couple, I have them map their past on a X-Y plane from birth to the current day. The exercise is not to fret over what has happened in their lives and to recall every detail but to pinpoint both highs and lows that have stayed with them. It doesn't take long, since the goal is just to mark those memories that we hold dear to us because of the happiness they bring into our lives or the sorrow we hold within. The higher the mark, the more joyful the occasion, while the lower the mark, the greater the pain. The idea is that all our lives contain both highs and lows—without them, we would not be living. This process allows couples to begin individually to look at their past to work on their present together. In this way their future begins to unfold as their narratives intertwine. A follow-up a year later with one of the couples revealed the impact of this exercise as the wife stated:

> The most memorable time during our wedding preparation was when we created a timeline of events that highlighted our lives: memories from childhood to adulthood. We marked significant dates and remembered special people in our lives, the highs and lows. Though I have known Matthew for fourteen years, I learned so much from his responses in this activity. The outcome revealed how much we both deeply care for our families. For me, this is the one that resonates. Every once in a while, we still talk about memorable events; and each day, we are getting to know more of each other. I also enjoyed hearing our personal ideas on faith and how God worked his way to bring us together. It was in this activity that we expressed our upbringing and differences in culture and religion.

## Intercultural Marriage

Marriage preparation allows couples to articulate their personal experiences as they begin to use their "rudders" in navigating their historical and faith narrative within a specific cultural context. While most tend to compartmentalize these areas of their lives or are even unaware of them, our memories are in a complex engagement within the individual. "One reason it's impossible to un-see trends is that our minds are engineered to seek out patterns and to assign meaning to them. Humans are a meaning-making species."[5] As couples realize that the stories of their lives are embedded within a context that is culturally conditioned, self-identification and self-awareness begin to surface. In many ways, this process is "easier" with those of different ethnicities than with European Americans (even though they, too, are a cultural/ethnic group). A reason for this is that European Americans may not see themselves as existing within an ethnic group or having a cultural identity in the way that other ethnic groups do. For example, a parishioner who prepares couples with the *Marriage in the Lord* program responded with a common perspective to culture as a person who did not have to reflect much on his own identity or heritage:

> When I consider my own cultural and ethnic heritage, I guess I would describe it as the "traditional" American (white), Protestant (Wesleyan) culture. It was mostly influenced by my family's church community. Since I was a third-generation American, I wasn't really exposed to any specific European ethnic heritage. There were only a few "family" recipes used in the kitchen. I was exposed to other ethnic heritages, traditions, and foods through friends with whom I grew up with that I remember most. It wasn't until I started dating my wife that I was truly exposed to other cultures, specifically the Mexican American and Catholic cultures.

Being white is as different and complex as being Latino, Black, Asian, and so forth; however, the dominant culture/identity often gets overlooked as another cultural group existing within this diversity. Rather, couples of differing backgrounds often default to the notion that they can simply be "American" and somehow this label reconciles the diversity of backgrounds. However, if we truly believe that being "American"—the so-called mainstream or the present way of being—comprises many cultures, ethnicities, identities, and so on, then the intercultural process must be part of this reality as well. Because of the complex dynamics involved in understanding one's narrative, couples will also sometimes default to a position of wanting to "just be Catholic." This, too—just being Catholic—is also culturally conditioned and requires a similar process of understanding how faith is expressed within each heritage and comes together in the lives of the couple, as illustrated in the following case.

Catherine and Peter are an intercultural couple that I had the opportunity recently to prepare for their wedding. As a side note, I had the "luxury" of preparing such couples for at least one year, a time frame many pastors will not have since most couples come to the church looking to get married as efficiently as possible. Thus, what I would have to cram into a minimum amount of time (six months), I was fortunate to be able to present the materials and develop relationships with the couples over a longer period. The length of time is important since it allows the couples to digest what is presented and for those preparing the couple to reinforce the intercultural nuances over several encounters. Young couples such as Catherine and Peter take time to realize not just the requirements of their lives together but what it means to have to map and navigate such a life together.

Peter is a European American Catholic who was marginally raised in the church, while Catherine is a Filipina American Catholic whose immigrant parents stressed the values of the homeland and the reasons for coming to the United States. Peter identifies as being Catholic but admits to being unfamiliar with the faith since it did not resonate with him over the years, with little reinforcement from his parents or his sphere of friends or environments at school, work, and especially the athletic pursuits in team sports that were important to him. Catherine sought to embody her heritage by being obedient to her parent's wishes. Whether or not Catherine realized it, she was actually engaged in a form of filial piety that included the religious observations of her parents. Growing up in such a manner, she made the Catholic faith a part of her identity as a Filipina American. At times, these two identities are inseparable since culture carries the expressions of faith and vice versa. Peter, on the other hand, did not necessarily connect the aspects of culture and faith in his own life story since his upbringing did not intimately connect the two. Added to that was his inability to see that being white meant belonging to a cultural group as well.

In our first session together, I asked the two to reflect on their life history with both culture and faith in mind. As Catherine and Peter went over their life graph, they had difficulties in making these cultural connections beyond racial categories. Thus, Peter did not initially identify any cultural conditioning in his own upbringing while Catherine saw her cultural understanding in Filipino celebrations, images, language, and so forth. At first, I took this couple to be culturally naïve since they could not go beyond racial affiliation. However, this so-called naiveté can also be seen in another way. Rather than the absence of cultural understanding as part of their cultural identity, both Catherine and Peter were unable to identify or verbalize their cultural heritage since this was the first time they had been asked to reflect on their lives in this manner.[6] Over time, they became more sensitive in identifying cultural connections even though the struggles to verbalize what they were pointing to continued. In the end, these conversations became more familiar and comfortable as the two were learning to navigate the cultural maps that began emerging in these conversations.

In order to address the couple's history, these discussions must be situated within the existing and emerging cultural contexts. Culture is the basket that holds the stories of one's life and the faith that has been expressed. I became keenly aware of this when I was preparing Catherine and Peter for their marriage. Peter (European American Catholic background) stresses the importance of being part of a team because of his involvement in water polo. As a player and now a coach, teamwork was always highly stressed, and success was conditioned by how well the group performed. Peter has transferred this "worldview" into other areas of his life, especially in his relationship with Catherine:

> I've been on a team basically my entire life. I thrive in that environment. I'm the first person to say that I'm not perfect. I have blatant strengths and weaknesses. I think this is why I love being part of a team, because your teammates have your back and you have theirs. As a collective group you are able to overcome obstacles you wouldn't be able to do yourself. I've been blessed to be a part of some extraordinary teams that have given me friendships that I cannot even describe with words. I think some of the most important characteristics of being a team player are loyalty and sacrifice. Loyalty in a sense that I know that I will stay loyal to the direction dreamed up by the team as a collective, and I know my teammates are committed to the loyalty as well. Sacrifice in a sense that I will put the team and its success ahead of my own personal benefit.

Catherine, on the other hand, values independence and personal achievement, especially in education. As a Filipina American Catholic, Catherine grew up with strong Asian values conditioned by her immigrant parents, with particular emphasis on academics:

> I have always been a very independent and academic person. Even since I was little I always did well in school, and reflecting back I rarely asked people for help. As a result, I carry an all-or-nothing mentality. When I set a goal for myself, I do everything I can to achieve it. Failure is not really an option for me. At times when I did "fail" in life, it was very foreign and uncomfortable for me. Ultimately, however, these failures only pushed me harder toward achieving my goals. My independence has made it so that I prefer to do tasks on my own, rather than in a group. If I am placed in a group-work environment, I tend to be the leader who delegates the task of the group so I know who is doing what.

In the past, these characteristics were considered one's personality and that when the lives of two people came together, they had to adjust, accommodate, and understand each other's quirks and personality traits. However, further conversations during the preparation process revealed that the stories of how their lives emerged were indeed culturally conditioned.

Peter never had the experience of being an "outsider" in church or society. He could easily fit into many situations. This is all part of white privilege, since the same barriers or limitations are not present within this population as with other ethnic groups. Thus, being part of a team is more easily achieved because one is accepted as such. Catherine's family did not have the same benefits, even though her own parents were highly successful doctors. As Filipino immigrants they naturally tended to stay within their own immediate families and with others like themselves. Growing up in this "isolated" community can condition a person to emphasize independence, as "fitting into so-called mainstream society" does not occur naturally. By going deeper into their life stories, the cultural foundations of their families shed light on their current relational dynamics.

Faith is also better understood in this cultural context as well. The temptation is to see faith independent of culture; however, both our inward reflections and our outward expressions are culturally conditioned. Regardless of whether we inherit another cultural religious expression or grew up within certain devotions, the engagement of such liturgical practices is an invitation to cultural engagement as well. As a child of Filipino immigrants, Catherine grew up Catholic, celebrating Sunday Eucharist within the dominant English-speaking community, but she was also exposed to Filipino devotions such as *Simbang Gabi*, an Advent novena in preparation for the Lord's birth.[7] The challenge is to see both encounters of worship within their respective cultural context and not just because of their association with a particular ethnicity other than white or mainstream. While many forms of worship that Peter engaged in were familiar to Catherine, these cannot simply be seen as universal since they, too, are affiliated with a particular European way of expressing the faith. Less common expressions of the faith by the wider church can be due to language or simple preference, which does not diminish their universal dimension. Commonality is found in the reception of Catherine and Peter by making such diverse customs that they grew up with as their own way of prayer as a couple. The symbolic image of the kingdom revealed in the sacrament of marriage should also be reflected in the wider church as various methods of praying and encountering the divine should never be relegated to only particular groups within the Body of Christ. The challenge for couples and the wider church is to see that all particular expressions of culture and faith become universal, a part of their being, when lived out with openness and equality.

Once personal and religious histories are mapped out and are acknowledged as being intertwined in the cultural context of a person, then the identity of the individual and couple can be understood as operative in any life situation that the couple needs to address. The importance of this cannot be understated since without this initial process, it is quite difficult for "new" cultural and religious expressions and identity to emerge as the two become one. This "merger" of life stories and beliefs within the context of a particular cultural understanding is not one in which a couple has the luxury of embracing personal and religious similarities and differences in a "monocultural" environment of the older generation. Today's intercultural couples have a similar task to any married couple of embracing each other's lives but within a cultural environment that is beyond a singular or "mono-" culture, with diverse layers of complexity. That is why cultural and generational navigation is important in any intercultural union.

*For Richer or for Poorer*

# Navigating the Hurt Trail and Foreboding Joy

Owning our story can be hard but not nearly as difficult as spending our lives running from it. Embracing our vulnerabilities is risky but not nearly as dangerous as giving up on love and belonging and joy—the experiences that make us the most vulnerable. Only when we are brave enough to explore the darkness will we discover the infinite power of our light.[8]

In mapping the past—both the highs and lows of our lives—individuals uncover and become better aware of both the hurts of their past and the joys of their achievements. The "hurt trail"[9] is where experiences continue to affect our lives and define us knowingly and unknowingly. At the same time, the highs in our lives—those moments above the graph—are indeed joyful moments that affect and define us similarly. Brené Brown speaks about the need to be vulnerable in order for our lives to become courageous and heroic in dealing with the past:

> I think we've lost touch with the idea that speaking honestly and openly about who we are, about what we're feeling, and about our experiences (good and bad) is the definition of courage. Heroics is often about putting our life on the line. Ordinary courage is about putting our vulnerability on the line.[10]

In my pastoral encounters, the hurt trail often has a greater influence in our lives than the joyful moments, no matter the quality and quantity within our past. Again, Brown mentions that the interaction of the "good and the bad" are constants in our lives and that "playing down the exciting stuff doesn't take the pain away when it doesn't happen. It does, however, minimize the joy when it does happen. It also creates a lot of isolation."[11] The reason for this is that the hurt trail continues to affect other areas of our lives if not properly healed. The hurt trail eventually makes its way to the blissful moments in our lives, making those moments fleeting or unattainable and not the true moments they ought to remain for us. An unreconciled hurt trail creates the "foreboding joy"[12] in our lives in which we cannot truly appreciate our happy encounters. What is needed then is compassion in both the healing as well as the sharing process of our lives:

41

# Intercultural Marriage

> Compassion is not a relationship between the healer and the wounded. It's a relationship between equals. Only when we know our own darkness well can we be present with the darkness of others. Compassion becomes real when we recognize our shared humanity.[13]

These moments of happiness and sadness are all situated in a cultural context, and addressing their impact becomes a lifelong task of reconciliation with and acceptance of oneself and one another. Thus, the cultural insights needed at this point depend on how one listens because she or he is aware of the cultural dynamics within and also operative in the other. Just as communication, financial, child-rearing, and other skills are being learned and put into practice in any marriage preparation process, cultural competency is also a vital part of this process. Without such navigation skills, the maps being created simply are not enough.

Navigation or gaining cultural competency is not about solving problems or righting the ship in a predetermined direction. In any relationship, the purpose of accompaniment is not about "fixing" the other or the situation. Rather, accompaniment is simply that, walking with the other regardless of outcome. The navigational skills provided in marriage preparation allow us to accompany the other as we realize our own cultural conditioning as well as the cultural influence of the other. Therefore, cultural competency is an important aspect in navigating the maps of our lives.

Cultural awareness is vital, for it tells us the needs of the couple and their starting point. Traditional marriage preparation programs address the couple with an inventory of challenges that couples will face. There is wisdom to this since marriages are marriages regardless of cultural backgrounds. Two people coming together to become one demands that a couple navigate similar challenges. Traditional marriage preparation programs are able to address a series of life issues in a methodical order based on previous experiences and are essential to this process. I invite all couples to engage as many programs as they are willing to, since they all provide some type of life skills involving navigation. However, the cultural dimensions are often overlooked for a variety of reasons. This, then, provides all pastoral leaders, clergy and lay, with an opportunity to engage the couples more deeply with the skills that couples acquired. Since most marriage preparation skills are acquired outside the context of the encounter with the clergy, work on cultural competency—putting the navigational skills into practice—provides an invaluable forum when marriage prep people meet with the couples on an individual basis.

Discussing the cultural context of where identity and faith reside allows couples also to articulate the challenges of their lives rather than the other way around, where they are told what challenges are most important. In most instances, the issues raised in marriage prep are similar and first done by the presenters regardless of programming, since similarities in marriages do exist. However, cultural awareness allows couples to voice their own strengths and weaknesses and to give the preparation process a different emphasis in conversation with the pastoral minister. Thus, beginning the marriage preparation process based on one's understanding of culture and how we make meaning out of our encounters directs conversations to where greater attention is needed. Both the traditional way of preparing couples and this intercultural emphasis are necessary. In fact, they complement one another as the cultural aspect provides an opportunity for greater depth than the materials covered in the traditional inventory approach.

It is this intercultural approach based on each person's own life experiences that provides the couples with the ability to create their own cultural reality in their future lives together. Without this preliminary engagement of their own life, the two becoming one intercultural reality is nearly impossible. Within this important movement is the process of reception and transmission so vital for the transference of our faith practices for the next generation. While the outward expressions of both the cultural identity and religious practices may be similar to those of the parents' generation, what emerges out of these conversations is a greater ownership of their lives as part of both a particular ethnic and faith community. This ownership often occurs after navigating the values of each person's heritage, especially in how the couple receives and interprets what their parents have passed down.

Catherine and Peter again illustrate this point as they grappled with the order of matrimony when it came to the eucharistic celebration. Originally, they decided not to include communion for personal reasons. While both grew up Catholic, they did not necessarily view the reception of the Eucharist as essential for the expression of their love for each other before the community. During this time, I asked the couple to further articulate the importance of this decision in their lives in order to explain this decision to their parents or to anyone else. While Catherine's parents saw the Eucharist as a crucial element of the sacramental commitment to each

## Intercultural Marriage

other and the church, Peter's parents did not necessarily feel the same way, since their level of commitment was not the same as Catherine's parents. This is not an uncommon situation, and many would not even see this within a cultural context but rather just an issue with one's faith. Regardless of whether one views the situation as cultural or not, articulating the rationale for someone else requires cultural nuancing. While it was easy for Peter to tell his family that their liturgy would not include the Eucharist, Catherine's family had much more difficulty with this initial decision. This was fine for the European American Catholic family whose faith practice and identification had little to do with Sunday Mass attendance, but for Catherine's Filipino family, a union without receiving the body and blood of Christ made little sense, since many Filipino Catholics held an inseparable identification of Sunday Eucharist with being Catholic.

In the process of finding ways of articulating their decisions beside the commonly stated reasons such as one partner not being Catholic or many guests attending not being Catholic, Catherine and Peter's attempt to articulate their desires actually led them to value this part of the wedding ceremony that they were at first inclined to neglect. Rather than celebrating their special day without the Eucharist, both Catherine and Peter took ownership of why they now wanted to include the sacrament. This conclusion was partly informed by their desire to respect the cultural values of the understanding of the Eucharist with respect to the Filipino culture, but it was now also a result of their own insights. In particular, Catherine and Peter saw the inclusion of communion as an important part of their own faith journey. Locating themselves somewhere in between the faith beliefs of both sets of parents, Catherine and Peter saw this as an important step in their own spiritual engagement and a bridging of their cultural backgrounds. This ownership was a positive sign in their preparation but not the end, as Peter was still discerning whether to receive the sacrament of confirmation before the wedding. Eventually, he decided that he was not ready for that step. Having the couple articulate certain desires helped bridge their faith because it forced them to start making bridges across their own cultural identities.

Another intercultural couple, Ella (Filipina) and Matthew (British), attend Mass together every Sunday. However, Matthew is not Catholic but from a different denomination and did not feel the need to convert from his Anglican roots prior to the wedding.[14] In part, it was his way of honoring his own upbringing in his English community and his family, who were still living in England. He realized that his identity and religious affiliation were connected, and to honor one was to honor the other. Again, ownership of each person's religious practices and beliefs was articulated through this process. Embracing each other's culture as understood by the other is important when it comes to cultural competency. Even when certain cultural practices are not performed, it was important for Ella to communicate what certain traditions meant to Matthew.

> I remember watching the documentary about the liturgy with multicultural images of the Holy Mass being celebrated around the world. This was very helpful most especially for Matthew as we both prepared for the Catholic wedding Mass. I had to explain some of the Catholic wedding rites, such as tying the cord and putting on the veil. Although we didn't do this ritual at our wedding, it was good for Matthew to hear about our sacred matrimonial tradition.

A year later, this couple still attends Mass together. They had figured out a way to pray together in the same space while at the same time respecting their diverse backgrounds.

It is important to note that preparation is not the completion of these processes in which the couple's lives are all squared away before their marriage date. Any preparation program is just the beginning stage, and the work needs to continue in all future endeavors. Likewise, growing in cultural competency for greater accompaniment—the navigating of our maps—allows for the intercultural realities to emerge as the couple's lives are lived out together.

# Discovery—a New Reality Created by Marital Unions

In his seminal work on Living Mission Interculturally, Anthony Gittins provides a simple definition based on common intuition: "Culture is about people-in-society, about how they live, and about how individuals and groups are both similar to and different from others."[15] Gittins further elaborates, "Culture, then, is (1) the [hu]man-made part of the environment; (2) the form of social life; (3) a meaning-making system; (4) social skin; and (5) an enduring social reality."[16] From this understanding,

## Intercultural Marriage

he creates relational frameworks of how different cultural groups came together in the past as well as future implications on how we must truly be intercultural. The rationale for this future insight is that relational models of previous interactions were not based on equality and mutual embrace. Rather, a dominant group often appeared in these relationships, thereby relegating the minority characteristics to a status as inferior to or inappropriate for Western society and thought. Thus, the less dominant cultural expressions such as language were not as valued and passed down because of their foreignness from the locations of origin.

In the United States, this often meant that European Americans within the English-speaking cultural setting welcomed others, but at the same time assimilated those newly arrived into what we often call "being American" without considering how such a reality emerged from the contributions of different European cultures within the immigrant experience. Rather than seeing this process as ongoing and necessary to fully reflect the fabric of U.S. society, the so-called American culture has remained stagnant and frozen within the European experience. The process of intertwining together personal stories of departure and resettlement along with the faith expressions that many European ethnic groups used to hold and maintain their cultural heritage is not as honored by Americans as other immigrants. For these immigrants, conformity to what has resulted in their past is still upheld as the ideal today.

The stagnation of this process for non-European cultural groups in various areas of the world led Gittins and others involved in building diverse communities to rethink the encounter of different cultural groups and reformulate what is needed within a truly intercultural context. What has emerged within this thinking is that the interaction of different cultures must not only take from what is best in one group or the other, but in the process of inheriting the richness of each cultural group a new reality emerges. In other words, the cultural context of a truly diverse community resembles the strengths and richness of one's individual heritage but can only be truly appreciated when a new cultural setting emerges from the mutual reception of the other, where equality becomes key no matter how dominant a culture is or how small it may be in its existence as a minority. "This is a culture in the making and, paradoxically, everyone within the new community will be an outsider, but each is able to become a *participating outsider* and to bring his or her particular culture to the emerging reality."[17]

Translating these intercultural models within the marital context helps couples navigate their own life map as well as embrace new discoveries when two people come together as one. According to Gittins, this is an intentional act that goes beyond goodwill or good intentions.[18] Avoiding such mapping in one's life usually defaults to embracing a vague identity created by external structures such as "being American" or, if neither is originally from the United States, then being "Asian," for example. In the end, these categories are not necessarily meant for new meanings to emerge, for they are generic categories. In addition, such relegation to a default notion of culture usually means that the less dominant culture or cultures will be set aside. In couples in which both members are non-European Americans, this can ultimately mean that neither cultural heritage will be truly embraced in order to fit the immediate situation of the couples themselves or in the subsequent generations to come. Such interactions are evident throughout the United States, where a combination of any two minority groups is often found. Neither culture becomes well expressed in the couple's lives and even less so in their offspring. This also means that the children will have much fewer cultural ties because of their parents' lack of engagement in the process of cultural encounters as well as the development of their own personal identity. For example, when I asked Catherine and Peter about their identity as a couple as well as their future children's, they were at a loss as to what this might mean. Their response is a natural one since their children will no longer be of one ethnicity—familiar to the parents but unique in their own right. However, by reflecting on how their own narratives are necessary for this intercultural process, they will at least be able to provide a road map for their offspring and be conscious of the challenges that are before the next generation.

The loss of linguistic skills becomes the most obvious; however, other cultural expressions, engagements, and identities are quickly set aside, eventually becoming lost and forgotten. Obviously, there is no right or wrong in these situations since these are the realities of life in our complex society today, as one Latina Catholic described to me:

> My entire family spoke predominantly English, with only the older generations speaking Spanish whenever they didn't want "little ears" to listen to what they had to say. Over the years I learned to speak, read, and write in Spanish through classes taken in school, but not with ease or total fluency. To look at me one may not be able to pinpoint my ethnicity/cultural identity, but that's how I prefer it. God made me in his image,

and for me, being a woman of God is the most important identifier of all.

*Amen!*

What is important to understand in these cases is that culture is expressed in a variety of ways and beyond just language proficiency. What is needed for one to better understand his or her own identity is based on what is remembered in their intercultural experience and the willingness to pass it on to others. In the church, we have always called this the reception and transmission of our faith—and culture can never be excluded in this interaction for "faith is—and can only be—expressed *culturally*."[19]

It is in sharing the narratives of our past that important issues can also be raised in a similar context. For example, when raising the identity of the couple and their future children, the issue of racism in our society, church, and even our families can be raised. Again, in my conversation with Catherine and Peter this important issue surfaced, and to my surprise, it was Peter who quickly illustrated an encounter he had with this even though he is white. He described how he better understood the alienation of being different when he first attended the Filipino gatherings of Catherine's family. He could sense their eyes and how they were careful to either include him or allow him to step out of the group. Naturally, this tension was lessened with each opportunity to spend time with the extended family. Through this conversation, the couple also realized the challenges facing their children one day since they could either be included in multiple settings or excluded because of the way they look. Thus, one of the advantages of addressing the intercultural nature within marriage preparation is that it allows for this difficult yet important conversation to be surfaced, especially since we as church or society have yet to fully understand the implications of today's unions.

A new reality emerges when Gittins's understanding of different cultural backgrounds coming together to produce a new reality is applied to the engaged couples. The "default" reality is the result when we avoid this work, especially in marriage preparation. Rather, a new cultural setting begins to emerge and will continue to grow when the couple comes together and realizes the opportunities and challenges of a new context that arises from the uniting of their lives. Within this context will be the incorporation of the personal and faith narratives that are realized in their unique cultural settings and that are so intertwined that they appear as a unified presentation. When the couple's individual narratives come together as one in their marital union, it must also be conditioned by a new cultural reality that represents the new life that is being forged. This new reality is the result of an intercultural process since what emerges is not simply portions of each side nor a simple choosing of what is in the couple's best interest. Rather, this new cultural setting of the couple's lives is an intercultural reality because of the mutual reception of each other regardless of what amount is agreed upon as being necessary for the couple's identity.

In the case of the Filipina and British couple, Ella and Matthew, they were able to articulate some of the intercultural elements of their lives together. Granted, this couple was a unique case since they were getting married later in life. However, the process of joining their lives and background still remains the same for all those engaging different cultural backgrounds. For example, Matthew, who had recently immigrated to the United States at a later age, sustained the greater culture "shock" because of the newness of Ella's Filipino heritage, while Ella had been engaging other cultures in the United States since she immigrated with her family early in life. Thus, Matthew had more of an adjustment and found himself "feeling overwhelmed" at times. Through their time together, however, he discovered how to "love patiently" as he realized his place in the "hierarchy" of Ella's family. He soon learned to navigate the network of Ella's parents (extended family, friends, and so forth) within his own network, which was more centralized on his own existence:

> We also explored our cultural identities and how we assimilate and enjoy the differences and the similarities. For me, a lot of that is becoming a part of a much larger, more tight-knit family. As an ex-pat who only sees my birth family occasionally, that's been a lovely anchoring experience.

Ella's realization was an interesting one as she had to "learn" to be comfortable speaking Tagalog in front of Matthew, especially in large family gatherings. While Matthew never felt left out because he did not know the Filipino language, it was Ella who had to become comfortable speaking in her mother tongue without feeling self-conscious.

What this couple illustrates is different from the default positions, even if it is agreed upon by the couple themselves, since the default position requires little engagement, awareness, struggle, growth, and so on, while the discovery of a new reality requires a certain understanding of cultural influences in one's makeup in relation to oneself, each other, and

God. Ella and Matthew continue to this day to learn to become comfortable about who they are in front of the other rather than relegating such a heritage to the past. In doing so, they are inviting the other to experience and become part of their heritage. Naturally, this new reality begins to emerge in marriage preparation and continues as a lifelong commitment in the sacrament of marriage.

# Conclusion

The reason why we cannot simply be "Catholic" is because our being requires that our identity cannot be dismissed, since faith is also culturally conditioned. After all, we are Roman Catholics. While such a distinction has often been seen as universal, it is because the particularities of our faith practices have been embraced by those outside. What becomes evident is the process of universality, that all cultures must exchange mutually the richness from their own tradition. Therefore, the particularities of our culture, ethnicity, and so forth all contribute to a universal embrace. There is nothing wrong with being "American" or "Catholic" if we realize that the European experience/context has led to such a distinction or ideal. If the dialogue continues whereby non-European American Catholics are able to contribute to the universal realities of our identity and faith, then such labels are valid and appropriate. Unfortunately, we as church or society have not understood the necessity that every group needs this space for the wider communities to reach together an intercultural understanding of our church and society.

The marriage preparation conversation begins with the importance of mapping and navigating our historical and faith reality. Thankfully, most marriage preparation programs address these two realities. While they may lack emphasis concerning the past as programs are geared for the future reality, they still refer to the stories of individual lives to move forward. This also applies when it comes to the faith narrative. One's upbringing and formation (or lack thereof) is needed to engage the couple in their current faith formation for the sacrament of matrimony. What intercultural unions today remind us of is that all marriages are culturally conditioned. In the past, this was overlooked because different ethnic groups tended to stay within themselves. However, even within every ethnic group, cultural differences still exist due to location, generations, life experiences, and so on. The current increase of mixed marriages in our society simply highlights the fact that many of these important factors in every couple were overlooked or taken for granted—that couples were thought to be aware of their situation and knew how to navigate them. Often in the past, cultural topics emerged as issues with the in-laws or in child-rearing practices, for example. With the increase of intercultural marriages, we now are more sensitive that these relational dynamics are all part of our cultural identity and must now be consciously mapped out by the couples themselves in order for them to begin navigating the complexity of such encounters.

Chapter Four

# To Have, to Hold, and to Celebrate

*Liturgical Interculturality in the Wedding of Melissa Hoang and Roberto Gonzales*

Ethnographic notes by Ricky Manalo, CSP

THIS CHAPTER observes the liturgical celebration of marriage between Melissa Hoang and Roberto Gonzales, which occurred on August 8, 2015, in Orange County, California, and the relationship between liturgy, culture, and the intercultural dynamics that emerged during the planning, preparing, and celebration of their wedding ceremony at Our Lady of Guadalupe Catholic Church. Emotional nuances surrounding cultural values and responsibilities were identified between Melissa and Roberto, as well as their exchanges with family members, friends, the formal liturgical guides who helped plan and prepare their liturgy, and throughout our formal conversations. Interculturality was also evidenced during the marriage liturgy's Responsorial Psalm, the *arras*, and the Devotion to the Holy Family in a way that collectively embodied the Second Vatican Council's vision to consider the cultural context of the wedding celebration.

## Vatican II, Liturgy, and Culture

While those who gathered for Melissa and Roberto's wedding might correctly surmise that the planning had been done months in advance, they most likely did not realize that the intercultural aspects of their ceremony were actually years in the making. Since the ending of the Second Vatican Council in 1965, a sequence of official, theological, and pastoral resources has sought to develop official and pastoral guidelines for the planning, preparation, and celebration of liturgies in local church contexts. This effort brought a breath of fresh air to parish communities as the reforms of the council recognized the pluralism of liturgical forms and cultural expressions.

After centuries in which the laity remained relatively silent in the pews,[1] Vatican II encouraged the assembly to participate actively in the liturgy once again, as we read in the council's very first document, the Constitution on the Sacred Liturgy (*Sacrosanctum Concilium*, hereafter, *SC*):

> Mother Church earnestly desires that all the faithful should be led to that fully conscious, and active participation in liturgical celebrations which is demanded by the very nature of the liturgy. Such participation by the Christian people as "a chosen race, a royal priesthood, a holy nation, a redeemed people" (1 Pet. 2:9; cf. 2:4-5), is their right and duty by reason of their baptism. (no. 14)[2]

The model for this liturgical reform was drawn from the classical or pure Roman liturgy of the eighth century, a ritual that was characterized by "a noble simplicity…short, clear, and free from useless repetition" (*SC* 34).[3] But in its promotion for full, conscious, and active participation by the entire assembly, *SC* also set forth some norms with regard to the local church context by first moving away from a "rigid uniformity" in cultural expressions that marked the period before Vatican II, and then calling us to "respect and foster the genius and talents of the various races and peoples" (no. 37).[4] So as to allow for "legitimate variations and adaptations," the liturgical books (such as the Roman Missal, the Rite of Marriage, and so forth) needed to be revised in order to meet the cultural needs of the local church, provided that the "substantial unity of the Roman rite is preserved" (no. 38).[5] Further, all subsequent cultural adaptations were to be approved by "the competent territorial ecclesiastical authority" (no. 39).[6] The openness to cultural expressions and the accompanying directives made its way to the section on the marriage rite (nos. 77–78), reaffirming "other praiseworthy customs and ceremonies when celebrating the Sacrament of Marriage."[7]

After the Vatican II promulgations, worship communities throughout the world needed to adjust to the reforms. This process and interplay between liturgy and culture—between the unity that is found in the official church documents and the diversity of cultural expressive needs of a local worship community—eventually became known as "liturgical inculturation." The noted liturgical theologian Anscar Chupungco defined this interplay as "the process whereby pertinent elements of a local culture are integrated into the texts, rites, symbols, and institutions employed by a local church for its worship."[8]

The Order of Celebrating Matrimony[9] (OCM) reflects much of what emerged from Vatican II with regard to liturgical inculturation by devoting the last section of its introduction to cultural adaptations of the wedding rite (nos. 39–44). In his book *Inseparable Love: A Commentary on the Order of Celebrating Matrimony in the Catholic Church*, Paul Turner provides a succinct summary of the cultural adaptations allowed in OCM:

> Regarding adaptations, (1) the formulas may be adapted and supplemented; (2) where options exist, more may be added; (3) the order of the parts may be adapted; (4) the consent may be obtained through questions; (5) the crowning of the bride or the veiling of the spouses may take place; (6) the joining of hands and the use of rings may be omitted or replaced; (7) elements of tradition and cultures may be adopted.[10]

In addition to Turner's book, there is a wealth of resources to help guide our efforts to inculturate our celebrations of matrimony.[11] We need to look collectively to official, theological, and pastoral resources when we guide intercultural dynamics in ecclesiastical settings or sacramental planning, such as the preparations for Melissa and Roberto's wedding.

# The Wedding of Melissa Hoang and Roberto Gonzales

Melissa Hoang and Roberto Gonzales were married in Our Lady of Guadalupe Catholic Church in Southern California on August 8, 2015. They were surrounded by approximately two hundred family members and friends, along with a retired bishop of Orange County who presided at their ceremony and another bishop who concelebrated. Melissa is Vietnamese American and Roberto is Mexican American. Both worked for the diocese at the time this book was written.

Before I met with Melissa and Roberto on October 22, 2019, I emailed them the same cultural inventory I had used with Nina and Kevin (see chap. 2), along with the same instructions given throughout the inventory. The inventory instructed the couple to select three cultures and cocultures that resonated with them out of a total of eighteen. Then they were to discuss their answers with each other. Afterward, Melissa and Roberto shared that together they chose only one cultural value, "family," as the overall lens through which they approached the OCM. This did not surprise me, since their Vietnamese and Hispanic cultural communities are often more "collectivist cultures," rather than singular or individualistic in nature. If you recall from chapter 2, intercultural theorists use the term *collectivist* to suggest how some culture groups have a stronger need to consider the goals and values of a larger group over and above any individual need or desire.

> Relationships with other members of the group and the interconnectedness of people play a central role in each person's identity. Putting community needs ahead of individuals, working as a group and supporting others, doing what is best for society, and maintaining the central role of families and communities are a few common traits.[12]

"Family" then became the overriding cultural lens through which Roberto and Melissa's marriage ceremony was planned, prepared, and celebrated amid a spectrum of liturgical roles and cultural considerations.

# Interculturating Liturgical Inculturation in the Celebration of Matrimony

Many people from various ethnicities, cultural backgrounds, and levels of liturgical expertise contributed to the planning and preparation of Melissa and Roberto's wedding day. The bishop who presided was first contacted, as well as the director of the Office of Worship for the diocese. Other liturgical experts included a Franciscan brother who was a specialist in liturgies in intercultural contexts; a music director who was an authority on Vietnamese Catholic liturgy; and an editor of Oregon Catholic Press (OCP) who was in charge of Hispanic ministry for this music publishing company. Together, they became an informal "liturgical committee" to balance and negotiate the official components and cultural possibilities of the OCM with Melissa and Roberto, their extended families, and shared ethnic communities.

Like politics, all liturgies are local or, in this case, intercultural in their context, because they all involve people interacting with one another. In this case, a variety of ethnic and cultural groups were represented by the couple: Hispanics, Filipinos, European Americans, baby boomers, Generation X, middle class, and other distinctions were all going to be part of the marriage, whether anyone planned for it or not. To some extent or another, each of these cultural groups express their own set of values and worldviews through languages, symbols, art, music, customs, and rituals before and during the wedding.

There is a variety of cultural identities *within* each worshiper, even if we don't always know about them or notice them. For example, I was born in Brooklyn. My father was Filipino, but my mother's parental heritage was Filipino and Chinese, with her father being specifically of Fujian ethnicity. Because I was born in 1965, I also relate to Generation X as my generational cultural group. My father was a medical doctor and I grew up in a relatively affluent suburban neighborhood in New Jersey, so I experienced many of the sociocultural practices and economic privileges of an upper-middle-class white suburban culture. So much so, I often relate more to this latter sociocultural group than to the Filipino heritage of my parents. Finally, I am a Roman Catholic male priest and member of the Paulist Fathers community. Each of those descriptors has its own distinct social culture, in addition to my cultural awareness, worldview, pastoral responsibilities, and clerical privilege inherent in the Catholic hierarchy.

In short, each of us holds individual and collective cocultural groups within which we claim some level of affiliation as we gather with others who are negotiating similar coexisting realities. A young, suburban African American female university student may find herself being welcomed at the doors by an Asian Indian elderly male who recently became a United States citizen; a young adult white male who is visiting from Indiana and who, on average, celebrates Mass once every three months might find himself sitting next to a single mother of two daughters, both of whom are playing with toys below the pew; a bouquet of roses that reminds one person of their wedding is a reminder of the miracle of Guadalupe for another. We are a church of signs and symbols where rain begins an ark adventure of renewal, quenches thirst in a desert, and serves as a call for God to be present.

Given all the possibilities for any one expression of faith, it is somewhat astounding to think that the worship in a church of so many people can be defined by one particular century or contained in one kind of music, gesture, or language. Yet somehow, because of our formation in a particular style of music, ritual, or worship, we may feel more comfortable in an experience that has been defined for us as "church culture," even though none of us lived in the eighth or sixteenth century. Worship events bring together a spectrum of intercultural encounters that take place in one location within a particular time frame of temporal boundaries and remain in flux as they are influenced by experiences "within, in between, and outside" official worship sites, such as a church building. Theological convictions and temperaments may challenge one another, yet the church remains united in one faith, despite any clash of cultures or conflicting ideologies.

Our liturgies involve coexisting identities. We are members of the one Body of Christ who celebrate our identity in the consecrated bread and wine on the altar. Meanwhile, we surround the altar as baptized members of the one Body of Christ, now present in the liturgical assembly, and "beyond" in the homes of those who are not physically present during our liturgies but remain an unseen part of the Body of Christ. The Communion of Saints adds yet another dimension to our existence together in many places, as well as all those who are held in prayer in the hearts of all the faithful. Thus, we share multiple and interacting cultural identities whenever we gather to pray.

The intricacies of interculturality become more apparent when we attempt to locate a starting point or, more likely, multiple starting points of cultural influences that are present during the planning and preparing of a ritual, such as a wedding ceremony. This is especially true for a wedding where influence comes not only through the church, but via commercial wedding expectations, family customs, and cultural traditions.

Do we begin with the official rite itself, the cultural traditions, the values of the engaged couple, or a pastoral decision that combines many of the anticipated outcomes? We may have different answers for each expectation, depending on our role or on what we recognize as most important, but we can also be conflicted by multiple responsibilities and levels of accountabilities. If we are presiding, helping to plan the celebration, or are a close friend or relative of the bride or groom, we could have our own ideas as to what we think is most important.

That is why it is vital to consider how our own culture, general experiences, and any personal bias might influence our interpretation of the OCM. Understanding our expectations is important before we meet with anyone, particularly when it involves a new cultural experience with multiple points of confluence that can support or derail efforts to incorporate interculturality into a ceremony.

For their part, Melissa and Roberto never considered themselves to be what I would call "liturgical experts" at the time of their engagement. They admitted certain limitations when making choices for music but deferred to those who were helping with their planning. At one point, Roberto referenced a conversation with members of their liturgy committee, saying, "They pushed us…[said in an agreeing tone]. 'Well, why *that* song?' Or 'Well, *that* song has some Vietnamese, [but that *other* song has] some Spanish.'"

In the end, the couple acknowledged how much they valued how the planning support helped them remain sensitive to the cultural worship of their parents and their ethnic heritages. Roberto explained,

> I think Melissa and I both…wanted to spend time on the liturgy because we had families who worshiped in their native tongues. So, my Dad and my Mom only go to Mass in Spanish. And Melissa's Mom only goes to Mass in Vietnamese. So, if they are brought into celebrating Mass in their own language, then we wanted to honor and create an experience that honored that reality.

Later on, he added, "We even joked that a lot of couples spend a lot of time on the dinner and on the reception. But we wanted to spend time on the liturgy because that's what really was important to us."

My conversations with Melissa and Roberto helped me realize how each of them learned to connect the various components of their own cultural experiences and liturgical roles in a way that led to integrated planning and preparing decisions. For example, even prior to their wedding planning, Roberto and Melissa often interrelated the values of both the liturgical tradition of the Catholic faith and the traditions, ethnic and cultural sensibilities, and values of their own families. Liturgical interculturality had been forming in their minds and imaginations long before the planning, yet their openness to learning from the members of the liturgical committee who were competent not only in liturgical but also in cultural matters resulted in a wedding ceremony that was interculturally rich with theological meaning and pastorally sensitive to the needs of all who were present.

# Examples of Liturgical Interculturality in the Ceremony

I asked Melissa and Roberto to name three moments, rituals, or parts of the wedding ceremony they felt demonstrated a proper balance between the official text of OCM and their own cultural heritages and family. After discussing the variety of options, they chose the Responsorial Psalm, the *arras*, and Devotion to the Holy Family.

## RESPONSORIAL PSALM

The Responsorial Psalm is sung between the First Reading and the Second Reading. The General Instruction of the Roman Missal (GIRM) states,

> After the first reading comes the responsorial Psalm, which is an integral part of the Liturgy of the Word and holds great liturgical and pastoral importance, because it fosters meditation on the word of God.
>
> The responsorial Psalm should correspond to each reading and should, as a rule, be taken from the Lectionary. (no. 61)[13]

GIRM also indicates a preference that the Responsorial Psalm is to be sung. Melissa and Roberto selected a psalm setting for their wedding that was composed by Đ`ông Dao and Rufino Zaragoza, OFM: Tv 33: *Các Bạn Hãy Nếm Thử* /Ps. 34: Taste and See/Salmo 33: *Gusten y Vean*. The text is based on Psalm 34 (33) and has a refrain in three languages: Vietnamese, English, and Spanish:

**Vietnamese:** *Các bạn hãy nếm thử và hãy nhìn xem, cho biết Chúa thiện hảo dường bao.*

Intercultural Marriage

**English:** *Taste and see, taste and see that the Lord, our God is good, that the Lord, our God is good.*

**Spanish:** *Gusten y vean, gusten y vean qué bueno es el Señor, qué Bueno es el Señor.*

The refrain consists of two musical lines that indicate that two languages are to be sung simultaneously. The upper line text is sung entirely in Vietnamese, while the lower line has two sets of text that can be sung interchangeably in English or Spanish. At any one time, the refrain can be sung in either Vietnamese and English or Vietnamese and Spanish. There are four verses that were printed out in the worship aid in each of the three languages.

Melodically, the setting is composed in a pentatonic scale, which is a traditional scale in Vietnamese culture and consists of five notes per octave (see musical score on the next page). The Vietnamese top line is the beginning of the entire refrain, followed by the second line, which begins on the second measure, and is sung in either English or Spanish. The entire refrain is an example of intercultural music making, as two or more melodic linguistic lines are not only sung at the same time, but also dialogue with one another. There are moments when both linguistic lines are sung simultaneously and when one or the other line takes the melodic lead, while the other line pauses and sustains a note as another line continues.

The result is a melodic interchange between all three languages and, by extension, all three cultural groups that the languages represent. This is also a good example of how the official text for Psalm 33/34 remained intact (unity), while the various cultural symbols successfully expressed the cultural values and traditions of the three ethnic communities (diversity). The singing of this Responsorial Psalm exemplifies liturgical interculturality through the concurrent interweaving of musical lines and the interchanging musical prominence between the cantors, musicians, and multicultural assembly.

# BLESSING AND GIVING OF THE *ARRAS*

The *arras* (coins) is an optional rite of Spanish and Filipino origin and consists of the priest first blessing a baker's dozen of thirteen coins to symbolize prosperity.[14] Afterward, the couple each takes turns to exchange the coins with the other. The rite symbolizes God's blessing upon the couple and the hope for an abundance of gifts and prosperity that will

*To Have, to Hold, and to Celebrate*

## Tv 33: Các Bạn Hãy Nếm Thử / Ps. 34: Taste and See / Salmo 33: Gusten y Vean

Đồng Dao and Rufino Zaragoza, OFM

**Refrain**

Vietnamese: Các bạn hãy nếm thử và hãy nhìn xem, cho biết Chúa thiện hảo dường bao.

English: Taste and see, taste and see that the Lord, our God, is good, that the Lord, our God, is good.

Spanish: Gus-ten y ve-an, gus-ten y ve-an qué bue-no es el Se-ñor, qué bue-no es el Se-ñor.

**Vietnamese Verses: Cantor**

1. Tôi luôn chúc tụng Chúa Trời
   lời hát khen Ngài
   không ngừng rộn trên lưỡi tôi.
   Trong Chúa hồn tôi hãnh diện,
   bạn nghèo nào nghe tiếng
   tôi mà hãy vui lên.

2. Dâng lên Chúa lời ca ngợi nào
   hỡi các bạn
   ta cùng hợp tiếng tán dương.
   Tôi đã cầu khẩn lên Ngài
   và Ngài cứu chữa những
   ai dập nát tâm can.

3. Nhìn về Chúa để các bạn lòng
   trí vui mừng,
   không khỏi hổ ngươi bẽ mặt.
   Kẻ khốn khổ kêu khấn Ngài
   và Ngài đã cứu thoát họ khỏi
   những tai ương.

4. Chung quanh kẻ sợ kính Ngài,
   này các Sứ Thần
   đóng trại để canh giữ họ.
   Thiên Chúa thật bao tốt lành,
   thật là hạnh phúc biết bao kẻ ở bên Ngài.

**English Verses: Cantor**

1. I will bless the Lord at all times;
   God's praises ever on my lips.
   My soul glories in the Lord,
   that the poor and lowly may
   hear and be glad.

2. Come glorify the Lord with me,
   as one we praise God's name.
   I sought the Lord and was heard;
   from all my fears the Lord has
   set me free.

3. Those who look toward God
   are radiant with joy,
   their faces free of all shame.
   When the poor cried out
   the Lord heard;
   and God rescued them from all
   trouble and distress.

4. The angel of the Lord
   encamps with them,
   delivers all who fear God.
   Taste and see the Lord is good;
   Oh, blest are they who seek
   refuge in the Lord.

**Spanish Verses: Cantor**

1. *A cada instante bendigo al Señor,*
   *lo alaba siempre mi boca;*
   *se gloría mi alma en él:*
   *que lo escuchen los humildes y se alegren.*

2. *Glorifiquen conmigo al Señor,*
   *ensalcémosle unidos.*
   *Le consulté y él me respondió,*
   *y de todas mis ansias me libró.*

3. *Contémplenlo y de gozo irradiarán,*
   *vergüenza no sufrirán.*
   *Si el afligido invoca al Señor,*
   *él lo escucha y lo salva de sus angustias.*

4. *El ángel del Señor está con sus fieles,*
   *protege a los que le temen.*
   *Gusten y vean qué bueno es él,*
   *dichoso aquel que busca en él asilo.*

Text: Based on Psalm 34 (33):2–3, 4–5, 6–7, 8–9. Vietnamese text and music © 1983, 2009, Đồng Dao. Published by OCP, 5536 NE Hassalo, Portland, OR 97213. All rights reserved. English: Rufino Zaragoza, OFM; Spanish verses adapted by Eleazar Cortés. English text, Spanish verses text, and music © 2009, 2010, Rufino Zaragoza, OFM. Published by OCP. All rights reserved. Spanish refrain text © 1970, Comisión Episcopal Española de Liturgia. All rights reserved. Used with permission.

be shared between them and others as they embark on their journey of married unity. It was a natural decision for the couple to include this rite in their wedding, given Roberto's strong affiliation with his Hispanic heritage, yet it can require an openness and invitation, or even a suggestion on the part of leadership involved in the planning, to help couples understand what is possible.

During the ceremony, the presiding bishop spoke the blessing prayer:

> Bless, + O Lord, these *arras*
> that N. and N. will give to each other
> and pour over them the abundance of your good gifts.

Then, Roberto took the *arras* and spoke the following, while handing them to Melissa:

> Melissa, receive these *arras* as a pledge of God's blessing and a sign of the good gifts we will share.

Melissa then spoke the same prayer, while handing the *arras* to Roberto. However, she surprised everyone by speaking the prayer in Spanish:

> Roberto, *recibe estas cartas como una promesa de la bendición de Dios y una señal de los buenos dones que compartiremos.*

Melissa explained, "I don't know if it was our idea, but it goes back to Paul [a member of the liturgy committee]....Paul [was] joking with us because Paul's wife is Anglo." In referring to the Responsorial Psalm, Paul, who is Vietnamese American, said to Melissa,

> Paul: "You know, it would be really awesome if I did the Responsorial Psalm with my wife, but have my wife sing the Vietnamese and I'll do the Spanish and English parts...and no one would anticipate that!" And the moment [the wife] started singing in Vietnamese, everyone started looking around and asking, who's singing? And then Paul did the Spanish part, and everyone asked, "Wait...who's singing [now]?" So [both Paul and his wife] were another intercultural

marriage, exemplifying what it really means to be intercultural!"

At one point, Paul's brilliant idea inspired Melissa and Roberto to do a similar intercultural exchange during the *arras*.

Melissa: "I'm sure at some point I thought, 'Oh, you know, if she was going to sing in Vietnamese I'm sure I could speak in Spanish for part of it.' But you know the other part behind it was…we talked about this idea about having our families understand the rite….I wanted our families to understand that I was speaking, or I was representing [their culture]….I wanted to say the *arras* in Spanish so that they understood that I really *meant* it, that it becomes meaningful to me as well. And I know that…most of them understand English: [but] to hear worship and their tradition in their own language? That's much more meaningful!"

## Devotion to the Holy Family

Melissa and Roberto both chose family as their overriding cultural value through which they approached the planning of the wedding ceremony. The sharing of the *arras* illuminated this decision, but family also informed their decision to include the practice of presenting flowers to a statue of Mary, the Mother of God. This ritual, known by its short title, Flowers to Mary, is not included in the OCM but is an enduring ritual for many cultural communities who regularly practice Marian devotions.[15]

It usually takes place after everyone has received communion and right before the presider prays the Prayer after Communion, as a Marian hymn is sung, such as Schubert's *Ave Maria*, and the bride alone presents flowers to a permanent statue of Mary or a statue set up for the occasion. Today it is more common to have both bride and groom participate in this ritual together.

Roberto knew that Flowers to Mary was not part of the OCM; nonetheless he asked the director of liturgy for the Diocese of Orange, about

## Intercultural Marriage

including it in the ceremony, since the director represented the Worship Office and official teachings of the church:

> Roberto: "I remember asking [the diocesan director of liturgy], 'To do the Mary thing...is that a thing?' Then in the weddings [in our parish]...they have a prayer to family [turning to Melissa] or something like that?"

Roberto did not reveal to me the director's exact response, but he shared that in Our Lady of Guadalupe parish there are three statues of Mary, Joseph, her husband, and the child Jesus, otherwise known as the Holy Family. This "already set placement" of the statue led to their conceiving this ritual through their own collectivist lens, as Roberto explained:

> Roberto: "How do we honor *the family*, instead of [just] Mary? Right? If our family is surrounding us and we're going to kinda *become* this family, [then] how do we honor the Holy Family by the way we celebrate?"

At one point, they also decided to replace the traditional flowers usually presented to Mary and instead, decided to burn and present sticks of incense.

> Roberto: "The connection was made that instead of flowers, [we would] light incense sticks!"

The use of incense sticks is quite common in traditional Vietnamese culture, particularly to venerate ancestors, and is a great example for how to include an intercultural collectivist ritual within an official liturgy. At the same time, using incense to venerate ancestors has been recognized as a formal practice in the Catholic Church.[16]

In their marriage ceremony, Melissa and Roberto carried a small pot of sand and invited both sets of parents to place their lighted incense sticks into it. Then they added sticks to honor their grandparents and great-grandparents who were not physically present with them. Together, Melissa and Roberto placed the pot in front of the statue of the Holy Family, as the assembly sang the hymn *Cầu Cho Cha Mẹ 2*/Prayer for Parents 2 composed by Phanxicô and Rufino Zaragoza.

# Conclusion: A Wedding Ceremony through the Lens of Interculturality

This chapter focused on the liturgical celebration of marriage and the dynamic processes of interculturality that were part of the planning, preparation, and wedding celebration of Melissa and Roberto. Their wedding demonstrates how the interactive dialogue between liturgy and culture remains an important challenge and gift of the liturgical reforms that emerged from Vatican II. Since that time, liturgical inculturation has been utilized to shape official church documents and resources. This undertaking allows for the Roman Rite and other rites of the church, such as the wedding ritual of Melissa and Roberto, to maintain integrity as the prayer of the church, while incorporating practices and styles of varying cultures to meet and respect the needs and values of their local church community.

Melissa and Roberto's cultural identities and those of the worshiping assembly were respected during the planning, preparation, and celebrating of the wedding, as well as the complexity of the cultural interactions throughout their planning process. The Roman Catholic tradition was also respected and maintained. My discussions with Melissa and Roberto revealed how difficult it can be to find a starting point for planning and preparing a wedding ceremony of shared cultures, yet the support they received to negotiate multiple cultural styles and affiliations served to make Melissa and Roberto's wedding an exemplary model to integrate an intercultural context for all Catholic rituals.

Chapter Five

# From This Day Forward

*Interculturality as an Eschatological Sign*

IN 2017, the *New York Times* published an article, "The Faces of Intermarriage, 50 Years after *Loving v. Virginia*,"[1] highlighting cross-cultural, intercultural, mixed marriages. In the past, fascination with such marriages involving spouses of different ethnicities might have been owing to the rarity of such unions due to legal restrictions, racial stereotypes, taboos, and so forth. Today's fascination with couples of different cultural backgrounds, however, is based on their commonality in society. More and more marriages involving individuals of different racial and cultural groups are occurring in our society according to the same *Times* article, which also reports a Pew Research study showing a fivefold increase since the historic landmark decision of *Loving v. Virginia* fifty years ago. Today, one in six marital unions are considered such, making it much more of a commonplace in our neighborhoods and churches. Whereas previous encounters with racial and cultural differences were always at a comfortable distance since one could enter into and out of such a diverse environment, today's encounters are much more intimate because there is no compartmentalizing or escaping this reality when it comes to intercultural unions, and especially for their children. Therefore, the new space formed by cultural hybridity challenges social and religious norms.

Just as these mixed marriages are creating a new and intimate way for cultures to come together, the church's embrace of being an intercultural reality is an innovation that is also eschatological—here, but not yet fully realized. God's reign continues to unfold through the necessary interactions between the church and the world. Thus, Vatican II allowed for events such as intercultural marriages to signal the Spirit's movement. A careful reading of how intimacy emerges from an intercultural encounter or setting, both in the time of Jesus as well as today, allows the church better to respond to the pastoral and social needs when people from various backgrounds come together.

# Intercultural Intimacy

Interculturality goes beyond coexisting with the other (multiculturality)[2] and creates new opportunities of how people come together. In *Fides et Ratio*, John Paul II emphasizes the gospel encounter with the Greek-speaking world as an example of the ongoing cultural encounters and the necessary task of inculturation (*FR* 72). Therefore, such encounters involve a process of change, whereby one's identity does not remain the same but is transformed and enriched.[3] Through a mutual embrace of culture, language, and peoples, deeper movements of intimacy occur as illustrated by today's marital unions. The coming together of what was previously unimaginable, or from situations that were prohibited in the past, continues to reveal the dynamic nature of relationships found in Judeo-Christianity—the intimate ways of interacting with one another as a reflection of our relationship with the divine. Thus, becoming an intercultural reality in both church and society is not just about the diversity of its members but, more importantly, the ways cultures and peoples are received as having vital contributions[4] and allowed to forge a new creation through the interweaving of their worlds as well as through the generations to come.

In *The Sacred and the Profane*,[5] Mircea Eliade speaks of this new space as territory that humanity occupies to reflect divine cosmology. In doing so, humanity continues to create as well as perpetuate religious connections generationally and culturally. "To settle in a territory is, in the last analysis, equivalent to consecrating it. When settlement is not temporary...but permanent...it implies a vital decision that involves the existence of the entire community."[6] For immigrant communities, such establishments in this country come in a variety of forms. However, intercultural marriages signify the ultimate method of establishment, as these unions, especially when it comes to their offspring, cannot return to a "homeland" or continue in the same manner as the initial cultural groupings. Rather, a new territory is created where, for Eliade, the sacred can also be revealed. In order for this to occur, both secular as well as religious communities must have a role in upholding interculturality. What is upheld as a new territory is that intercultural couples become an *imago mundi* in which their marital union is "symbolically situated at the Center of the World."[7] Theologically speaking, marriages bringing cultural differences together should not be seen as aberrations or rare occurrences but rather, they must be viewed as today's version of the communication with the transcendent.[8]

Thus, intercultural intimacy does not simply mean a physical connection found in spouses of differing backgrounds; rather, it refers to how the lives of two different people must come together to appreciate the differences even when they cannot be fully comprehended. In this encounter, a greater sense of the mystery emerges and is appreciated since one can fully comprehend neither the complete reality of the other nor the new life of coming together. Rather, the embrace of the unknown is what helps us become church in the mystical communion as Christ's Body. Thus, Eliade cites the Greek understanding of marriage as telos, consecration, and the ritual involved in bringing two people together reflecting that of the mysteries in which tension, danger, crisis is implied.[9] Within this chaotic atmosphere also lies the possibility for the mystery to reveal an intimacy with the divine within our faith tradition. Just as Christ's hypostatic union is a mystical union of the divine and human in the breaking of bread and pouring of the cup, the mystery that is created in intercultural intimacy brings humanity closer to divinity.

Just as Eliade focuses on the present in the creation of a sacred moment, Geoffrey Wainwright points to the Parousia—the imminent return of Christ in glory as the final union between humanity and divinity. The coming together of creation upon Christ's return creates a "new territory" with the ultimate consecration of what is being signified today. Wainwright laments the diminished expectation of the Parousia in many religious circles and, thus, the inability fully to appreciate current encounters with the divine. He notes that the eucharistic celebration as the heavenly banquet heavily focused on Christ's return and that once enough time had passed, the church "relaxed" this outlook.[10] Paralleling this loss was the absence of the role of the Holy Spirit in the West. The significance of both has led to a lack of understanding in the eschatological outlook, especially when it came to eucharistic celebrations or any other sacramental moment for that matter. Rather than recognizing the Spirit's activity and focusing our lives on the future consequences of the reign of God, the church's insistence on the past in the present moment hinders our readiness of what is still yet to come.[11] This "eucharistic *causative* value" is realized in the reconciliation present with Christ's Body—"for such a eucharist will be the occasion for the Lord to exercise the three eschatological functions of casting out from us in the judgment what is amiss in us, of uniting us closer to himself in divine fellowship, and of joining us together in common enjoyment of his presence and gifts."[12] All of these characteristics of the eschaton are reflected in the ways people of different cultural backgrounds come together in an unitive way.

The use of Wainwright's eschatological perspective helps illustrate that something more is possible when we reclaim our vision of the coming kingdom as well as the current actions of the Holy Spirit in the lives of couples and in the church. Through sacramental intimacy found in intercultural marriages, the church is more prepared to partake of the mystery of the kingdom of God by being present. Since the sacramental life requires all our senses, can we not "taste" what is before us and thus participate in some manner, creating an eschatological intimacy through intercultural unions, echoing communion in light of the eschaton?

> To taste is to try the relish; and to say that the eucharist provides a taste of the kingdom therefore allows us to express both the provisionally [*sic*] and yet the genuineness of the kingdom as it flavors the present.…This use of *taste* is much rarer in the eucharistic liturgies and the theologians than one might have expected; but its value as an expression for the relation between the "already" and the "not yet" is undeniable.[13]

# Intercultural Christianity from the Outset

From the very outset of Christianity, the commandment to go forth in Matthew 28 entailed a condition for the faithful that was not within Jewish religious or cultural purview. "Luke–Acts tells us that on the morning of Pentecost the Apostles received the Holy Spirit and were empowered to proclaim this new way of love to all humanity."[14] Thus, the spreading of good news has always been an intercultural one from its beginnings.

## Intercultural Marriage

Along with this commandment to go to those outside of the Jewish world, the Pentecost event also illustrates the cultural diversity of her members as "Parthians, Medes, Elamites, and residents of Mesopotamia, Judea and Cappadocia, Pontus and Asia, Phrygia and Pamphylia, Egypt and the parts of Libya belonging to Cyrene, and visitors from Rome, both Jews and proselytes, Cretans and Arabs" experienced the outpouring of the Holy Spirit (Acts 2:9–11). This infusion of many different cultures as part of the ongoing formation of the early disciples laid the groundwork for what was to come in fulfilling Christ's command to go and make disciples of all nations (Matt 28:19).

Rather than a static monocultural faith expression, the call to go forth gave way to a dynamic where faith would continually be influenced by new cultures encountered in the task of evangelization. Although the Jewish people attempted to maintain a strict exclusivity regarding faith and culture, their everyday lives spoke of another reality since the encounter with Gentiles could not be completely avoided. How else would the Pentecost event have occurred had it not been for the necessity of those with differing ethnic backgrounds coming together for the occasion? Neither was the outpouring of the Holy Spirit an unplanned event, since the day of Parousia corresponded with Jesus's ascension into heaven, nor was the location coincidental since the moment of conversion took place when people from different nations gathered in one place.

> From the margins Jesus initiates not a new center but rather a new movement of the Spirit that enables people to cross segregating boundaries and form a new human family….Galilee would never become the center, but it was the point of departure for the beginning of a new creation, as the Galilees today continue to be points of departure or new humanities to emerge.[15]

Thus, the beginnings of the church entailed both the embrace and mixture of peoples, cultures, languages, and so forth that constitute an intercultural community of believers, since from the moment the Spirit descended upon them, every culture and people was now included in God's reign with equality and dignity as the signature hallmark of those who followed Christ.

Overcoming the greatest cultural hurdle—miscegenation—was implicit in following Christ's example since it called both Jews and Gentiles together. Once abhorred as the ultimate violation of purity, intercultural unions and their offspring exemplify the Pentecost event and internally fulfill Christ's commandment of proclaiming the good news to all peoples. Transforming a community from a singular cultural mindset to one of inclusion is truly the work of the Holy Spirit, and it was a struggle for the early disciples as much as for those of us today.[16] However, the challenge of inclusion of others is not simply welcoming them into the fold. The inclusion in both Jesus's final words and in the outpouring of the Holy Spirit is to embrace a new reality in which other cultures influence in a way that creates new opportunities for growth. Therefore, the original encounter of others and their inclusion into the community of believers expanded the community's understanding of God's family.

These two occasions after Christ's crucifixion, death, and resurrection not only mark the outward expression of the church but also illustrate that such a community of believers can be realized only in the encountering of others within their cultural context. It also reflected their current reality as well as the one that was still yet to come. Otherwise, new members would have been restricted to Jewish rituals rather than allowed to hold on to their Gentile heritage. Although seeing the value of differing cultures seems to arise after Christ's resurrection and the Pentecost event, Jesus's own upbringing in the Galilean region reveals that this was not a new beginning in any way, but a vision of humanity conditioned by his humble beginnings. "God did not become human as a universal, but in a particularity of Jesus's life and praxis, which began in Galilee. From a Christian theological perspective, therefore, every particular human life can become a Galilean experience of divine disclosure within the world of actual things."[17]

Therefore, Jesus did not command a new vision foreign to him but intensified a vision that included his Galilean childhood as well as his adulthood ministry to the poor since "Galilee would forever be an integral part of the Christian proclamation of the Good News by Jesus Christ."[18] From his very beginnings of being like us, Jesus was exposed to many peoples and cultures already intermingling through the economic trade practices in the region. Galilee was not simply occupied by the Jews but also became a home for many foreigners who occupied the region for their own economic well-being. With such economic transactions, cultural practices must have also been shared with one another since trade forced people to interact on various levels. Since Jesus's ministry challenged the Jewish establishment, he was preoccupied with areas that were heavily Jewish in population and with the Jewish religious traditions.[19] However, since he also dwelt in the midst of the marginalized, he did not spend his days in entirely Gentile-free zones but engaged in "alien cultures."[20]

With every burgeoning economy, trade practices created new classes based on wealth as well as marginalizing many more in poverty. Growing up in a culturally mixed economic setting provided a privileged lens that would shape Christ's ministry to come. In particular, Jesus's upbringing within an impoverished environment provided the focus of his ministry echoing the prophetic voice of Isaiah to bring good news to the poor and brokenhearted (Isa 61:1). Therefore, Christ's message during his earthly ministry continually challenged the establishment—those who advocated for their privileged positions revolving around race and economic well-being—to bring to the forefront of society those marginalized by an elitist mindset. Within this message, however, there is also contained the prophetic voice not only of attending to the poor but also of what influenced Jesus in his upbringing—those surrounding him already living in an intercultural reality.

The challenge to the Jewish establishment to heed the cries of the poor contained within it the message of also breaking down the racial and cultural barriers within the Jewish notions of purity. Jesus's message was not a complete departure from Judaism but centered on those who were excluded. Thus, to be culturally mixed was not an exclusionary act but rather a privileged place of hearing the good news of God's reign. To have multiple heritages did not place people outside of divine mercy and grace but, rather, placed diversity in the center of God's reign. Why would Jesus simply confront one of the sorrows of his childhood and turn a blind eye to the other injustices that plagued the people whom he called friends and learned from throughout his life? Although publicly this may not have been called out in his ministry to the poor, it must have always been operating in the back of his mind. What Jesus encountered in Galilee through the events and people around him became his mission as the call to tend to the poor was also a command not only to accept those of different ethnicity and cultures, but, more importantly, to accept such interactions when embodied in a single human being. Thus, Jesus's intercultural commissioning at the end of the Matthean Gospel and the Pentecost event of gathering people from all the ends of the world was truly an intensification of his earthly existence.

In the Acts of the Apostles, the early church experience further exemplifies the need for intercultural encounters through the tensions brought about by the temptations to remain in a strictly monocultural reality. The conflict at the Council of Jerusalem (Acts 15:13–21) illustrates the struggles the early disciples had in not only proclaiming the message of Christ but, just as importantly, also imitating his way of life. The final resolution opens the way for the community to begin realizing the work on behalf of the poor and must also include the welcoming of all cultures because of staunch supporters like St. Paul, whose own diverse background as a Diaspora Jew made him more receptive to the Gentiles and their way of life.[21] Jesus's command to go forth insists that peoples and cultures are to come together in rekindling his memories of the Galilean environment where people from all around came together for better or worse. Now with the power of the Holy Spirit, the injustices resulting from such interactions of cultural differences would be transformed into a truly just community of believers in which faith is not devoid of culture but, in fact, allows people of different heritage to create a family of God as witnessed from the time of Jesus's childhood. Thus, the Pentecost event that acknowledged different ethnic groups as part of God's reign is now being called into a more substantial reality to correct the earlier version as witnessed by Christ in his Galilean upbringing. "In a world of *missio*, the missioner is called to make manifest God's promises in Israel and their realization in Jesus and the Spirit."[22]

# Intercultural Christianity Today

It is undeniable that the Second Vatican Council opened the doors of the church to the world. By doing so, a dialogue of sorts was under way as the church was to continue teaching the world, but now the world would also be able to "contribute to the better ordering of human society."[23] In particular, worldly events needed to be scrutinized as signaling the incarnation—Christ in the world—just as the church had been proclaiming from her inception. Through events that impact the daily lives of both Christians and non-Christians, the church would come to see the Spirit's continued formation of humanity. In certain ways, the U.S. Catholic experience continues the Spirit's mission with the influx of immigrants in our neighborhoods and churches from its very beginnings. As people of differing cultural and ethnic backgrounds moved into specific neighborhoods, the church also felt the influence of their presence—foreign ethnically but not necessarily in religious belief. Therefore, the ecclesial response to the changing demographics within a given parochial area was to embrace a multicultural church. This embrace was either a joyful occasion or one borne out of necessity. Joyful moments of inclusion occurred less often than the accommodation of the other out of parochial needs if we take our cues from society once again. Just as neighborhoods feared outsiders entering their premises, parishioners also often embraced similar sentiments since they lived in the areas most affected. Thus, joyful moments of inclusion are few and far between, since these required an equality that the United States has struggled for many centuries to achieve and continues to do so to this day.

Equality is necessary since the other entering our parochial boundaries must be seen with just as much dignity as those who are already established within them. In addition, to truly appreciate cultural and ethnic differences, the established culture and language must be seen as one of many so that the newly encountered culture, people, and language can be seen as a blessing and asset, so that their presence simply adds to the richness of our communities of faith as well as in our residential neighborhoods and workplaces. Without such acknowledgment involving the equality of people and cultures, the tendency is to see the other as inferior because of their differences. Rather than appreciating the richness that they encompass, they are seen as needing assistance. Thus, compassion arises from the transformation of pity through the aforementioned equality within the context of a Christian narrative.[24] To be compassionate because the other is new to the area, speaks a different language, and adheres to different customs simply means that both parties understand the position that the other is in because of previous encounters—either experienced personally or through acts of solidarity.

The latter acceptance of a multicultural reality out of necessity, however, is a much more common experience in the ecclesial landscape of the United States. Starting with missionary encounters with the indigenous populations on the Eastern Seaboard as well as the treatment of our Hispanic brothers and sisters on the southern borders, those differing from the Euro-American experience of faith were often looked upon with pity because of their "uneducated" and "pagan" ways. Thus, they were included into the Christian fold out of duty to the missioner's version of the gospel message. The perspective of seeing the other as inferior because of their unfamiliarity with European religious customs, language, and mindset continues to influence the reception of new immigrants and people of different ethnic groups, especially in areas of this country where they did not tread before. While some communities do celebrate the presence of Catholics of different ethnicities, their inclusion often is to sustain the dwindling numbers of the older populations. Inclusion that is not joyfully celebrated is often accompanied by demands upon different ethnic faith groups to adapt to English-speaking practices in both ministry and administration. Basically, those who do not "pray, pay, and obey" in a manner similar to English-speaking Catholics are impatiently expected to adapt to the ways of those already established in the pews.

Returning to Vatican II's insistence on a humble dialogue between the church and the world where the signs of the times are interpreted in the light of the gospel, this is of great concern still today. The church has looked to the changing demographics of surrounding neighborhoods to brace for changes in church membership. The multicultural approach that arose out of the necessity of including others into existing ecclesial structures allowed the wider church to understand the changing faces of those in the pews. Just as Hispanic, Asian, or Black families moved into new neighborhoods, the church also acknowledged the movement of similar ethnic faith groups entering the church doors. Diversity has been acknowledged by membership, but usually with groups or gatherings with little interaction with one another.

Just as in the past, the movement of differing ethnic groups with their religious practices continues to impact both church and society. Ongoing immigration along with political debates surrounding migration should once again indicate to the church that something more than just diversity is on the horizon. One factor changing the multicultural landscape of the past is the marital unions that are being created by different racial and cultural groups. These intercultural marriages visibly occurring both within and outside the church indicate not only the acceptance and establishment of diverse communities but, more importantly, the nature of interculturality. Whereas previous receptions of diversity hinted at acceptance and hospitality, today's changing landscape reveals the need to go beyond the multicultural norms of the past. Mixed marital unions reveal the need for more than just acceptance or hospitality; they reveal the need to take on the other's worldview, taste, speech, and so forth. In other words, we must be intimately connected with the diversity in our midst, echoing the intimacy of interculturality found in many newly created families. Intercultural marriages, therefore, force couples of differing backgrounds to create together a new way of being that does not reject or deny one culture over the other but allows for a new way of interaction, thought, speech and even approach to the divine, especially in the creation of new life between the two. Thus, mixed marriages are a sign of where the church is headed—the need to be able not only to accommodate diversity, but to embrace an intimacy of diversity where the traditional ways of being church are enhanced by the equality of every people and culture. This is within our reach if the other is seen with the same equality and dignity one sees in one's own ethnicity and cultural practices.

# Steps to Interculturality

While celebrating the increase of mixed marriages, the challenge is to place these unions as normative for the church as part of the intercultural reality that emerges from Jesus's entire life, the outpouring of the Holy Spirit, and Jesus's eventual return. When placed within this eschatological framework, contemporary struggles to embrace such realities as the unfolding of Christ's love for God's people has both immediate impact for local communities and for generations to come. This obviously poses quite a challenge since there are no concrete road maps, only signs suggesting the direction in which we must go, due to the complexities of immigration and the resettlement process as well as globalization. Therefore, the earthly lessons of Christ are important for our changing context. The steps that Christ took in his ministry as well as in the formation of his disciples to enter the intercultural space—the Pentecost event—are the steps that we still need to take today.

In proclaiming the reign of God at hand, Jesus's teachings and miracles regarding those on the margins contained within them the inclusion process of God's people. As today's faithful are called to grow in their humanity by partaking in their spiritual union with one another and God, the instructions they receive must contain within them the notion of intercultural intimacy. Liturgical preaching, faith formation instructions, and service to the poor must include within the actual words and actions the notion that people of different cultural backgrounds are welcome and necessary in realizing God's reign. Whether directly or indirectly transmitted, the understanding that God's reign includes their own experiences of living in a diverse population or in solidarity must always be part of the evangelization process. After all, the holy father has called the faithful to become missionary disciples in *Evangelii Gaudium*, where evangelizers must not only take on the "smell of the sheep" but, equally important, must have "sheep" willing to hear their voice (*EG* 24). In this apostolic exhortation, Pope Francis reminds the church that to be a missionary disciple is to go into our surroundings with the message of Christ's invitation to be part of his Body, the church. In doing so, this message is in imitation of Jesus's own earthly proclamation only if we keep before us the intercultural intimacy that he held in calling the people to come follow him.

Eventually, the cultural diversity as illustrated from Jesus's childhood to his death and resurrection must emerge as a visible sign of God's reign. Just as the Pentecost event was the visible sign of the new way God's people would gather together in worship, evangelization by contemporary missionary disciples must also make present an intercultural intimacy between our relationship with one another and with God the loving Father. The challenge of achieving this is much harder than the previous step of simply placing before us the experience of living in a diverse population or being in solidarity. In other words, the paradigm shifts necessary in maintaining a message within a message requires further transformation of our lives.

The creation of an intercultural intimate environment requires the similar steps that mixed-marriage couples undergo. What these unions teach us is that mutual respect of differences is a prerequisite for love to develop between people of differing cultures. A single culture, custom, language, and so forth cannot be perceived as being superior to another. If one spouse feels inferior because of his or her background, then love does not have an equal footing to truly come to fruition. Thus, the people of God must also take on the same disposition by seeing others of differing backgrounds as equals if they want to engage the other in their midst. The hurdle in today's church involves an ignorance of how ethnic differences must be seen equally. Rather than seeing English-speaking Catholics of European descent as one of many cultural groups within our diverse country, this particular group is often seen as the exclusive or primary model of being both American and Catholic.

Mutual respect can only be achieved when all cultures, regardless of their longevity within the United States, are treated as one of many and viewed as having a valuable contribution to both church and society. The result of the Pentecost event is not for the nations to become a singular culture, but rather to take their cultural differences in forging new expressions in worship. Respect for cultural differences allows for religious and cultural contributions to be embraced and not hidden away in shame for fear of belittlement. When the faithful can exhibit their cultural heritage as part of the wider church and not relegated to their own ethnic space, then this equality allows for an intimate sharing and weaving that enhances the life of the church.

A concrete example of this is how we celebrate certain feasts in our liturgical cycle. While European devotions become universal celebrations for the wider church, many ethnic celebrations outside the European context are categorized as being valuable only for a particular community. Even the great celebration of *Nuestra Señora de Guadalupe* is seen as a Mexican celebration when this Marian presentation is actually for all of the Americas. In some dioceses where Catholics of non-European descent are the majority, their particular celebrations are nevertheless still seen as their own devotion and not meant for others. For example, with more than eight hundred Vietnamese priests serving in the United States, how can the devotion to the Vietnamese Martyrs or Our Lady of La Vang simply be "their" celebration when so many of them are serving the wider church? Beyond this reasoning, when the faithful have given their lives in such great numbers such as in the case of the Korean Martyrs (103 canonized in 1984, 124 beatified in 2014), should they not be models for the entire church instead of being designated solely for Korean Catholics?

# Conclusion

Thomas Rausch describes the eschaton as more than just about the four last things involving death and judgment, heaven and hell.[25] Rather, the eschaton comprises all of salvation history. The relationship between God and creation, especially with humanity, is continually realized as a way of grounding the covenant of creation.[26] Furthermore, any relational aspects—especially in regard to interculturality—ground us in the larger covenant so that we can also live in loving relationships given to us in this moment as well as in the future promise.

As the complexity of intercultural unions continues to pose challenges to church and society, much more effort must be made by both in order to create an environment that is indicative of the eschaton—here and now, but not yet fully realized. This is not to say naïvely that intercultural marriages fare better than those not categorized as such. Factors that make marriage successful are applicable to all groups; however, normative intercultural encounters remind us once again of the need to take culture seriously in any relationship. In both church and society, we are just beginning to grapple with this reality, which has been too long taken for granted. For example, not until the 2010 U.S. Census did mixed marriages appear as part of one's ethnic identity. Thus, the previous notions of mixed marriages, which were considered along the lines of skin color (e.g., black and white), are no longer the so-called norm and more attention is now needed to understand better how these unions play an intricate role in realizing the reign of God.

Finally, if the church is called to missionary discipleship, this requires no less of us than it did in the New Testament period. First, we must resist the temptations of cultural exclusivity (e.g., the temptation to remain within a certain culture in such a way that alienates others in their midst who do not belong to that culture). Without the mindset of how our words and actions must always transmit the intercultural intimacy of God's reign—the reception of other cultures as containing valuable and necessary insights into that economy—different cultures will continue to come together in multicultural ways while still struggling to come together as one Body. Second, by acknowledging that the Euro-American experience of the faith is just one of several encounters by various groups who have been shaped by the immigration and resettlement process in this country, other cultures are then able to contribute to the wider church, adding to the dynamics that have fueled the church in the United States for centuries. If steps such as these are embraced, even imperfectly at times, this process would contribute to the church's experience of the eschatological reality promised and constantly being brought about by Christ.

# Conclusion

## *Look Now with Favor on These Your Servants*[1]

IN OUR INTRODUCTION both of us shared personal stories that captured how we first came to encounter interculturality in our own lives. Our collaboration throughout the process of writing this book became itself a study of interculturality between two theologians. At first, we recognized the shared cultural links between us: both of us are Roman Catholics of Asian descent; we have a passion for cultural studies; and we love to promote the intersection of theological reflection and pastoral concerns. But early on we also recognized distinctions in our approaches to theology, with one of us steeped in systematics and ecclesial history, and the other disciplined in ethnographic methodologies as a way to draw out new and emerging paradigms for theological reflection. We found ourselves continually interacting and negotiating the particularities of our own approaches to the questions surrounding intercultural marriage, which consequently (and at times, frustratingly) led to a handful of revisions of outline drafts. Thankfully, as the process unfolded, the content of this book eventually took shape, bearing the markings of "something new." The result was what we believe could be a welcome resource.

Our starting location was the Second Vatican Council, a watershed event that marked an ecclesial convergence of monocultural, multicultural, and intercultural relations between the Roman Catholic Church and the world, and between and among the various cultural communities that form the one Body of Christ. Our ethnographic interviews with Nina and Kevin, the couple who had been married for close to fifty years and whose engagement period occurred during the first ten years after the council ended, taught us about the complexities and nuances of cultural identities that occur between two people. The narrative strands that

*Conclusion*

emerged from those interviews highlighted how intercultural couples may, at times, maintain their own distinct cultural heritages while formulating new paradigms for articulating marital unity. We hope the model of Nina and Kevin teaches us that all intercultural relationships involve a process of continuous encountering "from this day forward," especially for younger couples who may be starting their initial stage of sacramental inquiry. And speaking of younger couples, narrative tools were employed again during the writing of chapter 3, where we heard the stories of Catherine and Peter, and Ella and Matthew. By drawing upon other experts on interculturality, we learned that intercultural relationships often involve relational frameworks that force us to rethink the encounters between dominant cultural groups (such as mainstream or European American cultural values that continue to shape the U.S. landscape) and minority cultural groups. With careful guidance, such encounters potentially become vehicles and models for mutual reception and respect. Our hope is that chapter 3 becomes an essential resource for all pastoral leaders involved in marriage preparation between clergy and engaged couples and lay leaders who regularly participate in marriage preparation programs. Chapter 4 brought us into the arena of liturgical studies and sacramental celebrations as we heard stories from Melissa and Roberto and how they planned, prepared, and celebrated their wedding. We discovered how such vibrant liturgies involve a host of intercultural dynamics that stem from family members to liturgical leaders and experts. The result was a liturgical paradigm (one of many) of an intercultural marriage ceremony that should be helpful to all those involved in liturgical ministry. Finally, chapter 5 offered a theological reflection on the sacramentality of Christian marriage—a theology that is not new but is being newly uncovered due to the intercultural nature of today's unions. These cultural exchanges are found in Christ's proclamation of the kingdom of God along with the mission to spread the good news to all nations. Thus, today's intercultural marriages continue to reveal the depth of God's love to all of creation—a mysterious love binding us in unity through our diversity.

Finally, it needs to be stated that this resource is not the last word on intercultural marriage, but only a starting point as we look to the future from this day forward. Our goal was to provide pastoral, liturgical, and theological starting points for dialogue that we hope will lead to new and revised models of how we approach Christian marriage today. As our world and our society increasingly become more complex with each new generation—and, in reality, with each new year that passes by—our final hope is that all married couples, pastoral leaders, and theologians may take our baton and forge new paths ahead, adapt some of our insights into their own local contexts, and create new theological insights that may contribute to the tradition of our Catholic heritage.

# Appendix A
## *Cultural Influences[1]*

## Framing the Learning Action

COCULTURES INCLUDE RACE, ethnicity, culture, nation of origin, gender, sexual orientation, age, physical/mental abilities, class, and religion. Your identity is shaped by the cocultures you identify with and why. The cocultures that are important in how you define yourself can change over time. For example, a twenty-five-year-old woman may not identify age as something that shapes her identity, and yet when that woman begins to age, she may identify age as an important part of her identity in that people relate to her differently. Similarly, white people may not identify race as important to their identity, while many racialized people affirm that their race shapes their daily lived experience and therefore is a large part of their identity.

Go through the list of cultures and cocultures below and describe how they influence your life.

- What impact do they have?
- How do you benefit or not benefit from being part of the particular culture or coculture?
- If you were describing your culture,
  - which cultures and cocultures listed below *had* the greatest impact on your life at the time of your wedding;
  - and which cultures and cocultures listed below *currently* have the greatest impact on your life today?

- Gender
- Age
- Ethnicity
- Social class/Income of family
- School
- Region/province, urban, rural

## Intercultural Marriage

- Race
- Sexual orientation
- Ability/disability
- Religion

- Family
- Language
- Friends
- Religion

- Political views
- Electronic media
- Social organizations
- Others

Reexamine the list and choose which cultures or cocultures you share with your spouse. In which cultures or cocultures do you differ from your spouse?

- Gender
- Age
- Race
- Sexual orientation
- Ability
- Religion
- Ethnicity
- Social class/Income of family
- Family
- Language
- Friends
- Religion
- School
- Region/province, urban, rural
- Political views
- Ethnicity
- Electronic media
- Social organizations
- Others

# Appendix B

## *A House of Prayer for All Peoples*
## *Matrimony between Catholics and Baptized Non-Catholics*

IN THE 1969 EDITION, the church was energized by Vatican II but had little time to reflect on the postconciliar document on marriage. Thus, "the first attempt at writing such an essay for a revised liturgical book" had a minimal introduction that many often gloss over.[1] Almost fifty years later, the Order of Celebrating Matrimony (OCM) represents the church's ongoing reflections as the introduction (*praenotanda*) has been greatly expanded—from the original eighteen paragraphs to now forty-four. The current introduction is a deeper reflection that relies upon conciliar documents and the richness found in Scripture and Tradition.[2]

Of special interest, "matrimony" is used instead of "marriage" to capture the broader religious context. These subtle yet important changes are essential to what is being demonstrated. While "celebrating" a life event is located within the moment of marriage, "matrimony" goes beyond a specific location and encapsulates a lifelong journey together.[3] "The United States Conference of Catholic Bishops hoped that putting the word 'matrimony' in the title of this book would set its Catholic meaning in relief against other usages of 'marriage' in the culture."[4]

Paragraph 36 of the recently revised Order reflects the church's development as well as tensions still involved in welcoming non-Catholics. Noted liturgist Paul Turner notes that this is not a new legislation, just one that has not always been observed.[5] Therefore, Catholics marrying baptized non-Catholics should avoid the distraction of disunity and have their union celebrated without Mass. Only with permission from the local ordinary can couples from differing faith traditions include the Eucharist.

> 36. If a Marriage takes place between a Catholic and a baptized non-Catholic, the rite for celebrating Matrimony without Mass (nos. 79–117) should be used. If, however, the situation warrants it, the rite for celebrating Matrimony within Mass (nos. 45–78) may be used, with the consent of the local Ordinary; but with regard to admission of the non-Catholic party to Eucharistic Communion, the norms issued for various cases are to be observed. If a Marriage takes place between a Catholic and a catechumen or a non-Christian, the rite given below (nos. 118–143) is to be used, with the variations provided for different situations.

## Celebrating Matrimony without Mass

A central rationale for matrimony without Mass is based on the unity signified in the Eucharist. Since reception of communion reflects union with Christ and the church, the nuptial blessing should ultimately reflect this. When such couples celebrate their union in the church, there is disunity when it comes time for communion. "Most importantly, the wedding is a celebration of the unity and equality of the two partners" through the church's welcome, readings, exchange of rings, universal prayers, and nuptial blessing.[6] Turner emphasizes that people attending such a wedding, along with the bride and groom, are on more equal footing by uniformly fulfilling "their function as a community that witnesses and prays."[7] Even though there are two options for celebrating matrimony without Mass, the second option, in which the distribution of communion occurs, is not an attempt to avoid the parts that may be foreign to non-Catholics. Rather, the distribution of communion should be reserved for those areas in which priests are not readily available.[8]

The eucharistic meal has always unified those gathered at the Lord's table. In *Doors to the Sacred*, Joseph Martos emphasizes this unity in the first three centuries of the early church even when the fellowship meal became a ritual stressing the sacrificial aspect of Christ.

> For the early fathers eucharistic worship was both an expression and source of Christian unity....In their eucharistic worship

*Appendix B*

they experienced unity with each other in the living presence of Christ: they experienced it because they believed it, and they believed it because they experienced it.[9]

Thus, unity is not simply a profession but a way of life. While the bride and groom consent verbally and experience this reality, the experience of eucharistic unity is incomplete due to the inability to receive Christ in his body and blood.

Similarly, the *Catechism* stresses this unity since the Eucharist completes our Christian initiation as well as making us the church (1396). While the common bond of baptism allows for the marriage celebration, the divisions are more painfully felt at communion (1398). Therefore, the church's guidance for matrimony without Mass is sensitive to what the Eucharist requires, and desires to maintain the joyful hope found in the baptismal bond of matrimony.

A liturgical discord also occurs as the inability to receive communion is not only limited to the couples but extends to family and friends. It is not uncommon that one side receives communion while others either wait or come forward to receive a blessing. "If the ceremony takes place during Mass, and only the bride or the groom receives Communion, it signals an imbalance at the very summit of the Liturgy of the Eucharist between the couple who have just been joined as one."[10] Coupled with this discord is the uneasiness of those in attendance of not knowing why actions such as standing and kneeling are required during the eucharistic prayers. Rather than being a moment of prayer that draws people into the memorial of Christ's death and resurrection, non-Catholics may feel further alienated from what is signified. Although this discord is not uncommon during Sunday liturgies, the OCM stresses the aspect of unity not for appearance's sake but for active participation and full communion.

Not every prayer of the church involves Mass. The church's prayer reaches its summit in the eucharistic celebration; however, this does not mean that Eucharist must be included with every sacred encounter. Though every moment of our prayer is in anticipation of full communion, special moments directed to this calling are needed to remind us of our limitation and, more importantly, our potential. For example, baptisms are often celebrated without Mass due to overwhelming numbers. Practical protocols are not the only reasons as each sacrament has its own value. How else could the church explain the separation of the sacraments of initiation to be experienced at different moments of people's lives? Renewal in the life-giving waters of baptism involves a lifelong journey with the community into which one is baptized. Periods of formation before sacramental encounters are important milestones in the faith journey. Therefore, all the sacraments are invaluable as they point to communion with the Lord and one another ultimately found in the Eucharist.

# Celebrating Matrimony with Mass

In *Amoris Laetitia*, Pope Francis calls for the proclamation of the gospel to those who are not regularly practicing their faith as well as to non-Catholics. For the pastoral minister, this opportunity comes not only during marriage preparation, but also in witnessing the church's celebrations. Therefore, rather than simply suggesting that couples forego the eucharistic celebration because of the disparity in their worship traditions, how best can we use this moment to promote the church's understanding of eucharistic communion? Such a discussion is complex and cannot yield identical results every time. However, the inclusion of such a conversation serves as a pastoral incentive to inform couples about the deeper unity of matrimony and how this is ultimately realized in communion—a goal for all couples regardless of faith backgrounds.

Pope Francis also advocates that couples be prepared for "a profound personal experience and to appreciate the meaning of each of its signs" (no. 213). If the couple understands why they are not able to participate in communion and yet comprehend the sacramental moment, should they not be encouraged to do so as a fuller sign of their potential lives together? "In the case of two baptized persons, the commitment expressed by the words of consent and the bodily union that consummates the marriage can only be seen as signs of the covenantal love and union between the incarnate Son of God and his Church" (no. 213). Since the love shared points to a deeper reality—Christ and his church—the presence of baptized non-Catholics provides another perspective that enriches the church.

Another liturgical occasion in which non-Catholics witness communion without raising the issue of disunity is found when candidates (baptized non-Catholics) are encouraged to participate in the liturgy as much as they can when the catechumens are dismissed during the Rite of Christian Initiation (RCIA). This rite recognizes the baptism already conferred on non-Catholics, binding them in a special way to the wider community

*Appendix B*

even when not fully initiated. This baptismal bond is fully recognized since Christians are not rebaptized.

Symbolic discrepancies have accompanied the church's development. Early followers listened to the word of God at synagogues and then continued at another location for a fellowship meal. Remembering Christ through the hearing of the word and partaking of the meal underwent a transitionary moment until they came together in our current celebration. Later sacramental developments, such as matrimony, took place both outside and inside the church to reconcile civil and canonical rituals. Not until the eleventh century did it become customary for weddings to take place near a church so that a priest's blessing could be received afterward.[11] Liturgy—the people's participation in "the work of God" (*CCC* 1069)—had its disruptions since the church's belief took time to be expressed in rituals (and vice versa). Thus, revisions of sacramental practices should not be viewed as a retreat. Those of differing Christian backgrounds whose weddings were relegated to convents, rectories, or separate chapels before Vatican II should not fear the return of such attitudes. Otherwise, the message of inclusion becomes blurred when couples are asked to raise their children in the faith. Proper instructions on what baptized non-Catholics can experience, yet not fully participate in, are important lessons in a person's faith journey.

Just as other sacraments do not include Mass, the church still maintains a fuller expression of the sacramental life when it does. Again, baptisms are encouraged to be celebrated within the Sunday liturgy so more parishioners can experience this saving grace and the visual benefits of the wider community for those bringing their children to the initial sacrament.[12] Since the church desires that families raise their children in the faith, non-Catholics are not excluded from this initiation. They are present as their children begin their faith journey toward the ultimate realization of full communion.

# Conclusion

One should not be too quick to enjoin couples in which one member is a baptized non-Catholic to forgo a wedding ceremony with Mass. The guidelines in OCM 36 are clear but also offer the option of appealing to the local ordinary out of pastoral sensitivity. This then places the weight not exclusively on the status of the couple but, rather, places equal weight on the marriage preparation. When the local parish journeys with the couple, teaching all the richness and symbolism of matrimony, the decision is reached through a process of prayerful reflection. If the change of terminology from "marriage" to "matrimony" signifies not just a moment but something that reflects their entire journey—before and afterward—then a more comprehensive vision must be presented.

# Notes

## Preface

1. *Tita* is the Filipino term for aunt.
2. In 2016, the United Conference of Catholic Bishops published the current English translation of the second typical edition of the Latin ritual for marriage. On the history of this evolution and translation, see Gilbert Ostdiek, "Evolution and Translation of the 2016 Marriage Rite," in *Catholic Marriage: A Pastoral and Liturgical Commentary*, ed. Edward Foley (Chicago: Liturgy Training Publications, 2019), 43–60.

## Acknowledgments

1. Simon C. Kim is particularly grateful to Jim and Kieko Schrode who supported an earlier ministerial campaign for young couples. Through retreats, seminars, and workshops, Simon was able to further identify the challenges and shortcomings in theological reflections, ecclesial discussions, wedding preparations, and ongoing conversations for these couples afterward.

## Chapter One

1. These four cultural groups included: (1) "those from European Catholic monopolies such as Italy and Spain, who wanted no change"; (2) "those from non-monopolistic countries (meaning either non-Catholic countries or Catholic countries with a formal separation of church and state) in Europe and North America, who prioritized ecumenism (or bettering relations with Protestants)"; (3) "those from Latin America, who prioritized economic justice and reaching the poor and unchurched in their

countries"; and (4) "those from Africa and Asia, who had a full range of ecumenical outreach and social justice concerns oriented toward helping the Church grow in their missionary countries." Melissa J. Wilde, *Vatican II: A Sociological Analysis of Religious Change* (Princeton, NJ: Princeton University Press, 2018), 6.

2. "The Council's overwhelmingly progressive outcome cannot be explained by such traditional sociological factors as power, resources, interests, or even popular pressure. At the beginning of the Council, conservatives had, through the Roman Curia, more formal power than did progressives and more of almost every type of resource we can imagine: money, institutional access, staff, even printing presses. And they had these resources concentrated precisely where the central decisions about the Council would take place, namely, the Vatican. If power and resources could explain the outcome of the Council, nothing much would have come from it." Wilde, *Vatican II*, 4.

3. Wilde, *Vatican II*, 7.

4. Vincent Ryan, "The Roman Rite of Marriage," *The Liturgical Review* 3, no. 2 (1973): 1, https://www.churchservicesociety.org/sites/default/files/journals/1973-Nov-1-8.pdf.

5. Ryan, "Roman Rite," 1.

6. Ryan, "Roman Rite," 1.

7. Orlando O. Espín, "Toward the Construction of an Intercultural Theology of (Catholic) Tradition," in *Tradition and Tradition Theories: An International Discussion*, ed. Thorsten Larbig and Siegfried Wiedenhofer (Berlin: Lit Verlag, 2006), 283.

8. Espín, "Toward the Construction," 295.

9. Espín, "Toward the Construction," 283–84. Italics in the original.

# Chapter Two

1. Some scriptural scholars prefer the term *interethnic marriage*. See Craig Keener, "Interethnic Marriages in the New Testament (Matt 1:3–6; Acts 7:29; 16:1–3; Cf. 1 Cor 7:14)," *Criswell Theological Review* (Jan. 1, 2009); David Rowe, "Marriage Counseling for Multiethnic Marriages," *The Journal of Biblical Counseling* (Jan. 1, 2004); and Willa M. Johnson,

"The Holy Seed Has Been Defiled: The Interethnic Marriage Dilemma in Ezra 9—10," *Colloquium* (Jan. 1, 2013).

2. *Race*, like all of the terms in this section, is a socially constructed term that is meant to express visible markers of difference for the sake of social categorization. In the past these differences were thought to be "biologically valid distinctions," but this understanding is no longer accepted. Instead, it might help to see race as "the causes and consequences of the socially constructed division of social groups according to their so-called race." See "Race," in *The Oxford Dictionary of Sociology*, 3rd ed., ed. John Scott and Gordon Marshal (Oxford: Oxford University Press, 2005).

3. If race is *biologically presumed*, then ethnicity is meant to differentiate social groups from one another through *culturally* constructed categories: "Individuals who consider themselves, or are considered by others, to share common characteristics that differentiate them from the other collectivities in a society, and from which they develop their distinctive cultural behavior form an ethnic group" ("Ethnicity," in Scott and Marshal, *Oxford Dictionary of Sociology*). Thus, members of an "ethnic group" may use a number of categories for differentiation. In addition to "race," these distinctions may include religion, politics, or, as in the term "Hispanic," language.

4. One area of interest is in the field of pastoral psychology. But even here, Marsha Wiggins Frame also bemoans the dearth of available resources. See her "The Challenges of Intercultural Marriage: Strategies for Pastoral Care," *Pastoral Psychology* 52, no. 3 (January 2004): 219–32.

5. Gretchen Livingston and Anna Brown, "Intermarriage in the U.S. 50 Years after *Loving v. Virginia*," Pew Research Center, May 18, 2017, https://www.pewsocialtrends.org/2017/05/18/intermarriage-in-the-u-s-50-years-after-loving-v-virginia/.

6. Kristen Bialik, "Key Facts about Race and Marriage, 50 years after *Loving v. Virginia*," Pew Research Center, June 12, 2017, https://www.pewresearch.org/fact-Chank/2017/06/12/key-facts-about-race-and-marriage-50-years-after-loving-v-virginia/.

7. "Framing and Learning Anti-racism," Calgary Anti-racism Education (Calgary, Canada: University of Calgary): (1) https://www.aclrc.com/personal-cultural-identity; and (2) https://www.aclrc.com/cultural-influences-handout. The list included gender, age, race, sexual orientation, ability/disability, religion, ethnicity, social class/income of family, family, language, friends, religion, school, region/province, urban, rural, political views, ethnicity, electronic media, and social organizations. There is also the option for the couple to write his/her own term that is not listed ("others").

8. There was a somewhat amusing moment when Kevin mentioned aloud that his first cultural value was gender/sexual orientation. Nina, somewhat surprised, interrupted before he continued and asked, "I just wonder why you have gender and sexual orientation there [in that spot]." Kevin answered, "Well, gender was important [at the time of their engagement] because I wasn't going to marry a guy!" Of course, Nina then realized that "gender and sexual orientation" was indeed one of the cocultures among the list of eighteen options and the mentioning of gender/sexual orientation did not necessarily mean they did not share the same cultural interpretive value. Thus, while she did not list this as one of her top three, this category was not a source of tension, conflict, or negotiation. For this reason, we turn to the other two cultural distinctions: religion and race.

9. In the Roman Catholic tradition, an "interfaith couple" refers to a "Catholic and a person who is not Catholic planning or involved in a mixed marriage." Other terms that are used include *mixed marriage*, which refers to a marriage "between a Catholic and a person who is not Catholic"; and *mixed-religion marriage*, which refers to the marriage between a Catholic and another baptized Christian person who is not Roman Catholic. Robert J. Hater, *When a Catholic Marries a Non-Catholic* (Cincinnati, OH: Franciscan Media, 2006), 10.

10. Caryle Murphy, "Interfaith Marriage Is Common in U.S., Particularly among the Recently Wed," Pew Research Center, June 2, 2015, https://www.pewresearch.org/fact-Chank/2015/06/02/interfaith-marriage/.

11. For a primer on Filipino Catholicism in the United States, see Stephen M. Cherry and Ricky Manalo, *A Treasured Presence: Filipino American Catholics* (Washington, DC: United States Catholic Conference of Bishops, 2020).

12. Susan Ting-Toomey, *Communicating across Cultures* (New York: Guilford Press, 1999), 67.

13. In the Filipino language, the term *Kuya* means "brother" and could be used as an address to an older male relative: e.g., brother or brother-in-law.

14. For a history of the sacrament of marriage, see Joseph Martos, *Doors to the Sacred: Vatican II Golden Anniversary Edition* (Liguori, MO: Liguori Publications, 2014), 405–61.

15. John P. Bartkowski, "Connections and Contradictions: Exploring the Complex Linkages between Faith and Family," in *Everyday Religion: Observing Modern Religious Lives*, ed. Nancy Ammerman (New York:

Convergent Books, 2020), 153. Quoted in Ricky Manalo, *The Liturgy of Life* (Collegeville, MN: Liturgical Press, 2014).

16. OCM 62.

17. OCM 11.

18. *Building Intercultural Competence for Ministers* (Washington, DC: United States Conference of Catholic Bishops, 2012), 9.

19. There is a host of available resources in the field of intercultural competence. We recommend the following. For a general introduction to intercultural communication, see A. Scott Moreau, Evvy Hay Campbell, and Susan Greener, *Effective Intercultural Communication: A Christian Perspective* (Grand Rapids: Baker Academic, 2014); in the field of interreligious/interfaith marriage, see Robert J. Hater, *When a Catholic Marries a Non-Catholic* (Cincinnati, OH: Franciscan Media, 2006); and Naomi Schaefer Riley, *'Til Faith Do Us Part* (Oxford: Oxford University Press, 2013). For pastoral leaders involved in marriage preparation programs and activities, consider *Building Cultural Competence: Innovative Activities and Models*, ed. Kate Berardo and Darla K. Deardorff (Sterling, VA: Stylus Publishing, 2012). Finally, The Intercultural Communication Institute in Reed College, Portland, Oregon, offers regular summer programs on this subject: https://intercultural.org/program/siic/.

# Chapter Three

1. John Gottman, *The Seven Principles for Making Marriage Work: A Practical Guide from the Country's Foremost Relationship Expert* (New York: Harmony, 2015), 11–16.

2. Gottman, *The Seven Principles*, 12.

3. The Gottman Institute, "Give a Story" (email received December 24, 2019).

4. Gottman, *The Seven Principles*, 28.

5. Brené Brown, *The Gifts of Imperfection: Let Go of Who You Think You're Supposed to Be and Embrace Who You Are* (Center City, MN: Hazelden, 2010), ix.

6. It is interesting to note how cultural roles, norms, stereotypes, and so forth are switched between Catherine and Peter. Through this intercultural approach to marriage preparation, I realized that the individualistic characteristic attributed to white Americans was a formidable factor in

Catherine's life and the communal aspect that we tend to associate with Asians was engrained in Peter's life. Thus, it is important for such cultural inquiries since commonly held beliefs of certain groups may not be true for particular individuals as well as distracting from the real work that intercultural couples need to embrace.

7. *Simbang Gabi* ("Night Masses") is a sequence of nine masses that are celebrated in the early morning hours from December 16 to 24. For more on this novena, see Ricky Manalo, "Deepening Advent, Widening the Circle: *Las Posadas* and *Simbang Gabi*," *Pastoral Liturgy* 43, no. 5 (September/October 2012), 5–9.

8. Brown, *The Gifts of Imperfection*, 6.

9. The hurt trail is used by David Allen to identify the past hurts that are still operative in our lives; see David Allen, *In Search of the Heart* (McLean, VA: Curtain Call, 2004).

10. Brown, *The Gifts of Imperfection*, 12–13.

11. Brown, *The Gifts of Imperfection*, 14.

12. Brené Brown uses "foreboding joy" to describe what happens when we do not embrace the vulnerable moments in our lives (i.e., the hurt trail); see Brené Brown, *Daring Greatly: How the Courage to Be Vulnerable Transforms the Way We Live, Love, Parent, and Lead* (New York: Penguin, 2012).

13. Pema Chödrön, *Comfortable with Uncertainty: 108 Teachings on Cultivating Fearlessness and Compassion* (Boston: Shambhala, 2002), 74.

14. See appendix B for more details on whether a couple should or should not be able to include the Eucharist when faiths differ.

15. Anthony Gittins, *Living Mission Interculturally: Faith, Culture, and the Renewal of Praxis* (Collegeville, MN: Liturgical Press, 2015), Loc. 55 of 270.

16. Gittins, *Living Mission Interculturally*, Loc. 56 of 270.

17. Gittins, *Living Mission Interculturally*, Loc. 45 of 270.

18. Gittins, *Living Mission Interculturally*, Loc. 45 of 270.

19. Gittins, *Living Mission Interculturally*, Loc. 55 of 270.

# Chapter Four

1. "The clergy prayed entirely in place of and in the name of the community. As a result, the faithful were only remotely involved and paid

attention to their own personal devotion. Communion appeared to be a private devotion without any special link to the Mass." Bernard Botte, *From Silence to Participation: An Insider's View of Liturgical Renewal*, trans. John Sullivan (Washington, DC: The Pastoral Press, 1988), 3.

2. Constitution on the Sacred Liturgy (*SC*): https://www.vatican.va/archive/hist_councils/ii_vatican_council/documents/vat-ii_const_19631204_sacrosanctum-concilium_en.html.

3. This is a clear reference to Edmund Bishop's classic, *The Genius of the Roman Rite*.

4. "Even in the liturgy, the Church has no wish to impose a rigid uniformity in matters which do not implicate the faith or the good of the whole community; rather does she respect and foster the genius and talents of the various races and peoples."

5. "Provisions shall also be made, when revising the liturgical books, for legitimate variations and adaptations to different groups, regions, and peoples, especially in mission lands, provided that the substantial unity of the Roman rite is preserved; and this should be borne in mind when drawing up the rites and devising rubrics."

6. "Within the limits set by the typical editions of the liturgical books, it shall be for the competent territorial ecclesiastical authority mentioned in Art. 22, 2, to specify adaptations, especially in the case of the administration of the sacraments, the sacramentals, processions, liturgical language, sacred music, and the arts, but according to the fundamental norms laid down in this Constitution."

7. "The marriage rite now found in the Roman Ritual is to be revised and enriched in such a way that the grace of the sacrament is more clearly signified and the duties of the spouses are taught. 'If any regions are wont to use other praiseworthy customs and ceremonies when celebrating the sacrament of matrimony, the sacred Synod earnestly desires that these by all means be retained'" (*SC* 77). The last phrase was taken from the pre–Vatican II book.

"Moreover the competent territorial ecclesiastical authority mentioned in Art. 22, 52, of this Constitution is free to draw up its own rite suited to the usages of place and people, according to the provision of Art. 63. But the rite must always conform to the law that the priest assisting at the marriage must ask for and obtain the consent of the contracting parties." (*SC* 78)

8. Anscar J. Chupungco, "Liturgy and Inculturation," in *Fundamental Liturgy*, vol. 2 of *Handbook for Liturgical Studies*, ed. Anscar J. Chupungco (Collegeville, MN: Liturgical Press, 1998), 339.

9. Available online at https://litpress.org/Products/GetSample/4641/9780814646410.

10. Paul Turner, *Inseparable Love: A Commentary on the Order of Celebrating Matrimony in the Catholic Church* (Collegeville, MN: Liturgical Press, 2017), 44.

11. In addition to Turner, see also Paul Covino, ed., *Celebrating Marriage: Preparing the Roman Catholic Wedding Liturgy*, 4th ed. (Portland, OR: Oregon Catholic Press, 2011); and *Catholic Marriage: A Pastoral and Liturgical Commentary*, ed. Edward Foley (Chicago: Liturgy Training Publications, 2019). Regarding cultural considerations, see Mark R. Francis, who collaborated with Rufino Zaragoza and the Federation of Diocesan Commissions to create *Liturgy in a Culturally Diverse Community: A Guide towards Understanding* (hereafter, LCDC); and Mark R. Francis and Arturo J. Pérez-Rodríguez, *Primero Dios: Hispanic Liturgical Resource* (Chicago: Liturgy Training Publications, 1997). Finally, for a resource on marriage customs that are celebrated throughout the world, see George P. Monger, *Marriage Customs of the World: An Encyclopedia of Dating Customs and Wedding Traditions*, vols. 1 and 2, expanded 2nd ed. (Santa Barbara, CA: ABC-CLIO, LLC, 2013).

12. *Encountering Christ in Harmony: A Pastoral Response to Our Asian and Pacific Island Brothers and Sisters* (Washington, DC: United States Conference of Catholic Bishops, 2018), 8. See also Geert Hofstede, *Culture's Consequences: Comparing Values, Behaviors, Institutions, and Organizations across Nations* (Thousand Oaks, CA: Sage Publications, 2001).

13. See http://www.vatican.va/roman_curia/congregations/ccdds/documents/rc_con_ccdds_doc_20030317_ordinamento-messale_en.html.

14. See Turner, *Inseparable Love*, 111–16; and Francis and Pérez-Rodríguez, *Primero Dios*, 104.

15. The presentation of flowers before an image of Mary could be found in the 2004 *Ritual del Matrimonia* in the Spanish-language edition of the 1990 OCM Latin edition, which was approved by the Conference of Mexican Bishops. See Edward Foley and Richard N. Fragomeni, "The Marriage Rites: An International Perspective," in *Catholic Marriage*, 73.

16. On October 2, 1964, the Vietnamese bishops presented an official statement on ancestor veneration, entitled "The Veneration of Ancestors, National Heroes, and War Dead." See *Sacerdos* 36 (July 1965): 489–92. This announcement officially recognized this practice in Vietnam, even though this had long been established officially in China and Japan as early as 1939. On April 12, 1974, more specific practices were clarified, including the use

of incense sticks: "Burning incense and lighting candles on the ancestral altar, and prostrating with joined hands in front of the altar or the repository of the ancestors are gestures of filial piety and veneration, hence permissible." There is a longer history of interplay between the venerations of ancestors in Roman Catholic worship contexts that go back farther to missionary efforts in China by the Jesuits, particularly Matteo Ricci, throughout the sixteenth to nineteenth centuries, otherwise known as the Chinese Rites Controversy. For a more detailed history and theology of the veneration of ancestors in Roman Catholic contexts, see Peter C. Phan, "Culture and Liturgy: Ancestor Veneration as a Test Case," *Worship* 76, no. 5 (Spring 2002): 403–30.

# Chapter Five

1. Sherly Gay Stolberg, "The Faces of Intermarriage, 50 Years after *Loving v. Virginia*," *The New York Times* (July 6, 2017), https://www.nytimes.com/2017/07/06/us/the-faces-of-intermarriage-50-years-after-loving-v-virginia.html?hpw&rref=us&action=click&pgtype=Homepage&module=well-region&region=bottom-well&WT.nav=bottom-well.

2. *Multicultural* refers to a compartmentalized society in which groups exist next to one another. See Frans Wijsen, "What Is Intercultural about Intercultural Theology?" *GEMA Theologi* 38, no. 2 (2014): 189. "In contrast, interculturality implies a mutually enriching and challenging two-way exchange among different cultures…moving far beyond mere coexistence 'to emphasize and make more explicit the essential *mutuality* of the process of cultural interaction on both the personal and social level.'" For more on the theological use of internationality, multiculturality, cross-culturality, and interculturality, see Roger Schroeder, "Engaging Our Diversity through Interculturality," *New Theology Review* 30, no. 2 (2018): 65.

3. Wijsen, "Intercultural Theology," 189.

4. In her examination of how communication of remote villages is connected through the intensification of globalization, Cristina Sepsi Soare concludes, "The quality of intercultural communication is based on how each understands, accepts and respects the cultural differences of others." See Cristina Sepsi Soare, "Interculturality and Globalization," *EIRP Proceedings* 4, no. 1 (2009): 749.

5. Mircea Eliade, *The Sacred and the Profane: The Nature of Religion* (New York: Harcourt, Brace & World, 1959).

6. Eliade, *The Sacred*, 34.
7. Eliade, *The Sacred*, 57.
8. Eliade, *The Sacred*, 58.
9. Eliade, *The Sacred*, 185.
10. Geoffrey Wainwright, *Eucharist and Eschatology* (Akron, OH: OSL Publications, 2002), 154.
11. Wainwright, *Eucharist and Eschatology*, 175.
12. Wainwright, *Eucharist and Eschatology*, 177.
13. Wainwright, *Eucharist and Eschatology*, 188–89.
14. Virgilio Elizondo, "Jesus the Galilean Jew in Mestizo Theology," *Theological Studies* 70 (2009): 277.
15. Elizondo, "Mestizo Theology," 277–78.
16. Lee highlights a tense and conflictual atmosphere due to cultural interactions in the Galilean region, especially when it came to the symbol systems of Jerusalem. However, this tension must be interpreted within the context of first-century Judaism's intracommunity struggles to understand whether Jesus was calling his disciples into another way of life. See Michael E. Lee, "Galilean Journey Revisited: *Mestizaje*, Anti-Judaism, and the Dynamics of Exclusion," *Theological Studies* 70 (2009): 392–93.
17. Sean Freyne, "The Galilean Jesus and Contemporary Christology," *Theological Studies* 70 (2009): 297.
18. Freyne, "The Galilean Jesus," 284.
19. Freyne, "The Galilean Jesus," 285.
20. Freyne, "The Galilean Jesus," 292.
21. Freyne, "The Galilean Jesus," 291.
22. William R. Burrows, "Intercultural Formation for Mission: *Missio Ad et Inter Gentes*," *SEDOS Residential Seminar Arricia* (2007): 3.
23. Second Vatican Council, *Gaudium et Spes* (1965), no. 39, in *Vatican Council II: The Conciliar and Postconciliar Documents*, ed. Austin Flannery (Collegeville, MN: Liturgical Press, 2014).
24. For more on the Christian movement from pity to Christian compassion, see Paul M. Blowers, "Pity, Empathy, and the Tragic Spectacle of Human Suffering: Exploring the Emotional Culture of Compassion in Late Ancient Christianity," *Journal of Early Christian Studies* 18, no. 1 (2010).
25. Thomas Rausch, *Eschatology, Liturgy, and Christology: Toward Recovering an Eschatological Imagination* (Collegeville, MN: Liturgical Press, 2012), xiii.
26. Rausch, *Eschatology*, 19.

*Notes*

# Conclusion

1. Taken from the Nuptial Blessing: "Look now with favor on these your servants, joined together in Marriage, who ask to be strengthened by your blessing. Send down on them the grace of the Holy Spirit and pour your love into their hearts, that they may remain faithful in the Marriage covenant" (OCM 105).

# Appendix A

1. Inventory adapted from "Stand: Framing and Learning Anti-racism": (1) https://www.aclrc.com/personal-cultural-identity; and (2) https://www.aclrc.com/cultural-influences-handout.

# Appendix B

1. Paul Turner, *One Love: A Pastoral Guide to The Order of Celebrating Matrimony* (Collegeville, MN: Liturgical Press, 2016),4.
2. See Federation of Diocesan Liturgical Commissions (FDLC), *This Sacred Bond: A Pastoral Companion to The Order of Celebrating Matrimony* (Washington, DC: USCCB, 2016), 18, for a detailed list of sources in the *praenotanda*.
3. Turner, *One Love*, 2.
4. Turner, *One Love*, 2.
5. Turner, *One Love*, 51.
6. Turner, *One Love*, 51.
7. Turner, *One Love*, 51.
8. Turner, *One Love*, 53.
9. Joseph Martos, *Doors to the Sacred: A Historical Introduction to Sacraments in the Catholic Church* (Liguori, MI: Liguori, 2014), 247.
10. Turner, *One Love*, 51.
11. Martos, *Doors to the Sacred*, 425.
12. Martos, *Doors to the Sacred*, 203.

# Index

Anglo/White/European Americans, 4, 10, 11, 36, 37, 39, 40 46, 48, 56, 62, 79, 83, 95
Arras, 4, 52, 59, 60, 62, 63
Asian, 10, 11, 16, 36, 39, 47, 56, 75, 80, 96, 98, 103

Christ, 12, 25, 33, 34, 40, 44, 53, 57, 68, 69, 70, 71, 72, 73, 74, 76, 77, 79, 80, 81, 86, 87, 88, 89, 95, 98, 99
Christianity, 67, 69, 73, 100
Congregation for Divine Worship, 4
Constitution on the Sacred Liturgy/Sacrosanctum Concilium, 1, 4, 54, 97
Cross-cultural, 66, 99
Cultural encounter, 2, 5, 7, 10, 35, 46, 47, 48, 51, 57, 66, 67, 68, 70, 71, 72, 74, 79, 80, 81
Cultural humility, xi, 6, 8, 33
Culture, 2, 5, 8, 9, 10, 11, 14, 15, 16, 20, 21, 22, 29, 31, 36, 37, 38, 39, 40, 43, 44, 45, 46, 47, 48, 49, 52, 54, 55, 56, 57, 58, 60, 63, 64, 65, 67, 70, 73, 74, 75, 76, 77, 79, 83, 85, 96, 99, 100, 103

Devotion(s), 4, 29, 40, 52, 59, 63, 78, 97
Diversity, 2, 3, 4, 5, 8, 29, 32, 34, 36, 54, 67, 70, 72, 75, 76, 77, 81

Engagement (marital), 8, 9, 12, 13, 22, 26, 33, 58, 80, 90
Eschatological, 66, 68, 69, 100
Ethnic, 2, 3, 4, 11, 12, 13, 14, 28, 29, 30, 34, 36, 39, 43, 46, 56, 58, 60, 70, 73, 74, 75, 77, 78, 79
Ethnicity, 14, 19, 40, 47, 50, 56, 72, 76, 83, 84, 93
Ethnographic, 9, 22, 23, 26, 27, 52, 80
Eucharistic, 43, 68, 69, 86, 87, 88

Filipino/a American, 10, 14, 15, 21, 38, 39, 44, 56, 94

Hispanic(s), 10, 11, 55, 56, 62, 75, 93, 98

Identity, 6, 10, 11, 13, 16, 20, 22, 23, 26, 28, 31, 34, 36, 37, 38, 40, 43, 44, 47, 48, 49, 50, 51, 55, 57, 67, 79, 83, 101, 103

Immigrant(s), 3, 15, 28, 34, 39, 40, 46, 67, 73, 74, 103
Inculturate, 54
Intercultural, 1, 2, 3, 4, 5, 6, 7, 8, 9
Interculturality, 5, 9, 52, 57, 58, 59, 65, 66, 67, 68, 75, 76, 78, 80, 81, 99
Intercultural marriage, 3, 4, 5, 9, 11, 12, 16, 19, 22, 26, 34, 51, 52, 53, 56, 63, 65, 66, 67, 68, 69, 75, 76, 77, 79, 80, 81, 93
Intermarriage, 11, 16, 93, 99
Intimacy, 67, 68, 69, 76, 77, 79
Inventory, 13, 17, 22, 23, 32, 42, 43, 55, 101

Jesus, 36, 64, 67, 70, 71, 72, 73, 76, 77, 100
Jews/Jewish, 69, 70, 71, 72, 73, 100

Korean, 78

Latino/a, 36, 47
Lazo, 4
Liturgical inculturation, 8, 54, 55, 65
Liturgical reform, 1, 5, 53, 54, 65
Liturgy, 1, 2, 4, 44, 45, 52, 53, 54, 56, 58, 59, 62, 63, 64, 65, 87, 88, 89, 91, 95, 96, 97, 98, 99, 100

Mapping, 28, 30, 31, 32, 34, 35, 41, 47, 50
Mass, 18, 44, 45, 56, 58, 86, 87, 88, 89
Matrimony, 3, 4, 12, 22, 26, 29, 30, 43, 50, 54, 55, 85, 86, 87, 88, 89, 90, 97, 98, 101
Minority, 46, 81
Monocultural, 1, 2, 29, 40, 70, 73, 80
Multicultural, 1, 2, 3, 34, 45, 60, 74, 75, 79, 99
Music, 10, 56, 57, 58, 60, 97, 103

Parousia, 68, 70
Preparation, 16, 17, 22, 23, 26, 27, 28, 29, 30, 31, 32, 33, 34, 35, 36, 39, 40, 42, 43, 45, 46, 48, 50, 53, 54, 55, 65, 81, 88, 90, 91, 95

Race, 1, 2, 3, 5, 6, 7, 10, 11, 13, 16, 18, 19, 47, 48, 50, 53, 66, 67, 68, 70, 71, 72, 74, 75, 76, 77, 79, 83, 84, 89, 93, 94, 95, 96, 97, 99, 101
Racism, 18, 19, 48, 93, 101
Rite, 1, 4, 5, 12, 23, 24, 45, 53, 54, 57, 60, 62, 63, 65, 86, 88, 91, 92, 97, 98, 99

Sacrament, 3, 4, 5, 9, 11, 12, 24, 26, 29, 32, 33, 40, 44, 50, 87, 88, 89, 94, 97, 101

*Index*

Sacramental, 22, 23, 24, 43, 54, 68, 69, 81, 88, 89, 97
Second Vatican Council/Vatican II, 1, 2, 4, 5, 12, 31, 52, 53, 73, 80, 100
Spanish, 10, 47, 58, 59, 60, 62, 63, 98

Tradition, 7, 16, 24, 50, 54, 58, 63, 65, 68, 82, 85, 94
Traditions, 10, 19, 23, 29, 30, 31, 36, 45, 57, 58, 60, 72, 86, 98

Vietnamese, 55, 56, 58, 59, 60, 62, 63, 64, 78, 98

# About the Authors

As a theologian of culture, Simon C. Kim reflects on the generational movements of people as well as the development of their faith expressions away from the homeland. He reflects not only on his own experience of church and identity as the impetus for his theological reflections but just as importantly, how initial immigrant experiences are constantly in a creative tension between the life transmissions of the older generation to the younger along with the reception into diverse spaces.

Ricky Manalo, CSP, is a member of the Missionary Society of St. Paul (The Paulist Fathers), a composer of liturgical music, and a liturgical theologian. His academic interests lie in the intersection of everyday worship practices, sociology of religion, culture, and ethnography. In addition, he is a theological consultant on Asian American Catholicism for the United States Conference of Catholic Bishops. His writings reflect a pastoral sensibility with the goal of creating spaces for dialogue and implementing strategic plans.